from Pew to Pulpit

A personal story of God's grace and guiding hand, which led a small boy from a pew in an inner Belfast church to preaching in pulpits across Northern Ireland.

HUGH McALLISTER

First published November 2022

ISBN: 978-1-8381889-7-9

Designed & Published by Cedric Wilson
Email: cedricwilson@live.co.uk

ENDORSEMENTS

George Hilary,
Retired Pastor, Lisburn Christian Fellowship

I have known Hugh McAllister for over 30 years, initially as member of the LCF congregation, but then as a trusted friend and gifted fellow church leader. Over the years I have learned to appreciate Hugh's down-to-earth and home-spun wisdom, no doubt springing from and moulded by his no frills upbringing in Belfast.

Hugh has an eye for detail most of us would miss, a quest for godly lessons from the ordinary in life and a desire to encourage and inspire faith in us all. This book is an expression of this desire.

Rev Mervyn Ewing,
Retired Superintendent Minister, Lisburn & Dromore Circuit

I first met Hugh McAllister in 2014. From the outset I realised that he was a man who wanted to do things right. He was part of the leadership in Lisburn Christian Fellowship, but was contemplating leaving there to follow a nudge by God's Spirit to re-enter the Methodist Church. This was to pick up a thread of a previous calling earlier in his life, when he served the church as a Local Preacher. He felt that God had reawakened this desire and wanted to test this to see where it would lead. His humility shone through, and it was clearly evident that God and service were central in those initial conversations.

Very early on in our conversations it was apparent that Hugh was passionate about his relationship with the Lord Jesus and wanted more than anything for others to have the same experience. He is a very competent and thoughtful preacher and leader of worship, allowing everyone in the congregation the space to discover more of God for themselves. He is a man of integrity and profoundly honest as you will see as you read his book. It has been a joy to walk with him part of the way and an inspiration as he allowed the Holy Spirit to fashion and mould him as a man of God. As he has immersed himself into serving God as a Local Preacher in the Methodist Church, many doors have been opened across the country. Truth be told it's a rare thing to meet people who leave a lasting impression like Hugh did on me.

Rev Eleanor Hayden,
Superintendent Omagh & Fintona Methodist Circuit

I first met Hugh when I was the superintendent minister of the Pettigo and Irvingstown Circuit. He and his wife Hilary turned up as visitors one Sunday morning, a not unusual occurrence during the summer months. As with all visitors they were warmly welcomed and stayed to enjoy a cup of tea after the service. Later I discovered they had recently bought a caravan in Kesh and were looking for a church to attend in the area when staying at their caravan. I was delighted that they decided to attend Pettigo Methodist and became regulars, building rapport and creating friendships with myself and members of the congregation. To my surprise, a little while later, the Rev Mervyn Ewing, their minister from Lisburn, called me on the telephone regarding Hugh and his desire to re-establish his call as a 'Local Preacher.' This telephone call was quickly followed by a 'letter of recommendation' from Mervyn.

Needless to say, I and the congregations in Pettigo and Irvinestown were delighted and quickly scheduled Hugh into the preaching plan, where his insightful, direct and sincere style of preaching was well received. On my move to the Omagh and Fintona Circuit, as superintendent minister, I was delighted that Hugh agreed to serve on its preaching plan and later, in addition, the Upper Erne circuit, when I was supervising a new probationary minister. Several years later, Hugh continues to provide a wonderful service to God, sharing his preaching ability and giving generously of his time. I am thankful that he walked through our door and for his abilities and gifting which are used to the glory of God.

It's amazing the way God helps us constantly discover new avenues of service to one another, new opportunities to further His Kingdom and new ways in which we can make known His love. May God bless this book and may it a means of encouraging many on their journey of faith.

Rev David Turtle,
President Designate of the Methodist Church in Ireland

'From Pew to Pulpit' wonderfully reminds us that we are shaped by the people we meet and the places we inhabit and that God, because of His mercy and grace, is always at work to draw us to Himself. Hugh artfully immerses us into his story in an account which is both intriguing and inspiring. As he recounts his journey towards deeper commitment and service to God in a variety of contexts, he does so with honesty, humour and as a fellow traveller through the joys and trials of life. His story, combined with insightful reflections on a number of passages of Scripture, draws attention not primarily to Hugh, but to the beauty and love of His Lord and Saviour Jesus.

Rev Jim Rea,
Former President of the Methodist Church in Ireland

I am delighted to commend Hugh McAllister's story. Much of it resonates with me as I grew up in the streets of north and west Belfast. My late father was born only yards from Hugh's early home on Cupar Street.

I first met the eighteen year old Hugh in Upper Falls Church during my friend Robert Bradford's ministry and remember Jack Robinson and Jim McCormack affectionately. They all ministered in what was to become a frontline for violence in 1969 and the early 1970s. Hugh has a Barnabas personality, always seeking to encourage others. Suffolk was a flash point with regular violence and harassment by Republican paramilitaries. Hugh's father with others contended to retain the Methodist Church witness, to build bridges between the communities, but sadly this proved impossible.

This book plots Hugh's life experience in Belfast after the 2nd World War with its relative poverty, followed by living alongside community conflict in Suffolk and his call to preach. In the book, it is clear that Hugh's supreme loyalty is to the Lord Jesus Christ and to share the good news of the gospel wherever he goes.

ACKNOWLEDGEMENTS

I want to acknowledge a number of people who helped me during the process of writing and shaping this book. Their support, input and guidance encouraged me to find the space and perseverance, not just to write it, but write it in a way that tells my personal story of becoming a preacher in, I trust, an easy to read and encouraging way.

Firstly, I want to thank my wife Hilary and daughter Ellen. Hilary allowed me time and space to sit at my computer to think and write, when I am sure she needed and wanted to get out and do some shopping or visit friends. She has been a constant means of support to me since we both committed our lives to Jesus at same time in our living room on Easter Sunday evening in 1975. Ellen, who is an English teacher, took the time and effort to edit the book for me, ensuring that my spelling and grammar were correct and that my phraseology was understandable and appropriate.

Secondly, I want to thank my long-time friend George Hilary, who was the pastor of Lisburn Christian Fellowship when I attended it. George, on many occasions in recent years, when we have met and chatted over coffee, suggested that I should write a book based on the insights God gave me from every day events. It is he, along with the Holy Spirit, who sowed the seed of writing a book which started the whole process of. George has been a constant source of encouragement over the years.

Thirdly, I need to thank the Rev Mervyn Ewing, who was the superintendent minister of the Lisburn and Dromore Circuit when I came back to Methodism, seeking to take up my lapsed roll as a lay preacher within the Methodist Church. It was he, as a result of his trust in my calling, who was instrumental in opening up not one, but many doorways across Northern Ireland for me to begin preaching again within the Methodist Church. Without his faith in me I may never have been allowed to begin this journey.

Lastly, I would like to thank Cedric Wilson, the publisher of the book, for his professional, yet very personal, input. Cedric helped guide me through the writing, publishing and marketing of the book and gave invaluable advice on its style and layout during the writing process.

FOREWORD

This book has been written not for any financial gain or worldly kudos, but rather to share some thoughts and reflections that I believe God imparted to me as a means of encouraging, inspiring, challenging and renewing ordinary people in their everyday lives. My prayer therefore is that something contained within the pages of this book will bring blessing and inspiration to others.

It is worth saying that I have received no formal theological training, apart from some fundamental study when I was preparing to become a local/lay preacher within the Methodist Church during the late 1970's. As a result, it is hoped my language is down to earth and, I trust, easy to understand and comprehend.

Any profits derived from the sale of this book will be directed to 'Christians Against Poverty'. This is because I have seen firsthand the financial and emotional transformation the charity can bring about through their non-judgmental practical help and guidance in terms of debt management. Their intervention allowed a close family member to turn their financial difficulties around and become debt free and financially sound, as well as alleviating the stress and anxiety they were under. As Saint James said, "Faith without works is dead".

CONTENTS

CONTENTS

THE ROAD BEFORE SALVATION

I was born on the 16th May 1952, in 141 Cupar Street, Belfast. This was a relatively long street which ran from the Falls Road at one end, to the Springfield Road at the other, easily identified by the Orient Bar which was situated on the corner of the Springfield Road and Cupar Street. My grandfather (Joe McAllister) frequented this establishment, maybe too often at times, as it was only a short walk from his home in Cupar Street. I often wonder if this played a part in the decline of his business and his change from a being a successful businessman and boxing promoter, to someone in receipt of benefits

Orient Bar, corner of Cupar St & Springfield Rd

and still residing in Cupar Street in his final years. I do know, because of one incident I still vividly remember, where he fought and almost choked my father, that at times drink affected his personality and thinking. Little did I know then as a young boy that drink would plague my life for a while in my late teens and early twenties.

Our house in Cupar Street was typical of those in many Belfast streets, being a two up, two down, red bricked Victorian terraced house with a 'back yard,' which housed the outside toilet. Since my parents moved house when I was still very young, I remember little of this home. I do know that my mother never really settled there as, on their honeymoon, someone broke in and burgled the house, stealing all of the wedding presents that she and my dad had received. I do however vaguely remember my dad and a neighbour trying to catch a rat which had gotten into our Cupar Street house and was hiding behind the free-standing kitchen cabinet. Maybe this is where my fear of rats and mice came from.

My dad's parents (Joseph and Maud McAllister) and their family lived on the same street, in number 305. My memories of their house, due to frequent visits as a young boy, remain vivid. It had a front parlor, used mainly for my grandfather's business. In the hallway, on a wooden table, was a large black dial telephone which neighbours were allowed to use. Because of this I always thought it was a public phone. As a phone in the 1950's was a luxury item, the

big black telephone always fascinated me and I loved to use the dial, hear the sound it made winding back and pretend I was phoning someone. The living room fairly small, not helped by the amount of furniture in it. Granny always seemed to sit near the open coal fire, beside the large television set. Due to her love of cats there were always kittens running about and climbing over the furniture. Of the living room was the scullery (kitchen), containing not much more than a large sink, a small worktop and a few cupboards. Linked to this was a wooden framed extension which contained an assortment of random items. One thing which always puzzled me was a gas mask which hung on the wall, obviously a relic of the Second World War. I never found out how or why it got there.

Although I visited my grandparent's home on a regular basis I never ventured upstairs and still have no idea what the bedrooms looked like.

My mum and dad were essentially working class, so no 'airs and graces'. Mum worked as a weaver in the Ulster Weaving Company, following her mum and older sisters into this working environment. Although born in Glasgow, when her father was working there, she grew up mainly in Blythe Street, which again was (and still is) a long street just off Sandy Row in Belfast. I remember the street had a large area of derelict land, the result of bombing during the Belfast Blitz. Mum's family (Hugh and Annie McCallum plus her four sisters) lived in the very last house, near the railway track and Blythe Street Primary School, which I attended. The house had three bedrooms, which were obviously needed to house mum, her four sisters and my grandparents. I have many fond memories of this house, as on Saturdays all the family would congregate together, aunts and uncles, plus my numerous cousins.

One thing that troubled me for a long time was why all my aunts, one at a time with my granny, retreated to the 'wee room', which was off the living room. I later discovered it was to settle accounts over the various 'clubs' they were all in (i.e. shop credit clubs, not

From left; Grandfather Hugh, Uncle Billy, my Dad & Uncle Johnny

3

Watching Orange Parade Belfast

Sandy Row arch which grandfather Hugh helped erect

sporting ones). When I got married my wife became a 'member', buying goods on credit from stores like Gilpins of Sandy Row and Gordons and making weekly payments via my grandmother.

As far as I can recall no-one was overly politically minded, but we all went every 12th July to watch the Orangemen parading. It was always fun to shout out to those family members and neighbours we recognised and hand over cold drinks to sustain them on the long walk to 'The Field' at Finaghy. The family always occupied the same spot on the lower Lisburn Road, just above Bradbury Place. Frequently, relations of my grandfather would come from Canada to stay for the 12th of July celebrations, creating a party atmosphere in their Blythe Street home.

My dad trained as an electrician and obtained employment in the Short Brothers and Harland Aircraft factory. He was resourceful because I recall during a period of unemployment he put his electrical skills to good use by making and selling sets of Christmas tree lights to earn much needed money. We, plus many of our neighbours, owned a set of these. For many years at Christmas they hung on our artificial Christmas tree, looking like a long string of multi-coloured egg cups. The Christmas tree didn't look much better, resembling a collection of stiff black bottle brushes stuck together in a manner loosely resembling a tree shape.

Father with Aircraft factory workers

Father with mum when he was Mayor of Lisburn

After I was born dad became the sole bread winner as mum had to give up work to look after me, the done thing for mothers in those days. Dad was a conscientious worker and ultimately rose to the position of Quality Auditor within Short Brothers and Harland, where he worked, I think, all of his working life. His claim to fame came when he was elected Mayor of Lisburn in 1989, a position he held for two years. This was something he was very proud of but he never let the position go to his head. When he died as a result of a road traffic accident it was gratifying to read the headlines in a local paper which referred to him as 'The People's Mayor'.

Cupar Street

As I said earlier, I have scant memories of living in Cupar Street. This is because we moved house when I was very young to 3 Coolbeg Street, which was off the lower Donegal Road, just above the Belfast City Hospital. Sadly the street has since been demolished, making way for the City Hospital's multi-storey car park. It was a typical Belfast Street of red brick Victorian terraced, two up two down, houses. Although still with an outside toilet in the back yard, we had the luxury of having a small room off the scullery (i.e. kitchen) which contained a bath. However, I don't think it had running hot water and I can't ever remember being in it. Under the stairs there was a little cupboard (the coal hole) which was used to store firewood and coal. My lasting memory is that it was infested with 'clocks' (cockroaches) which we usually found wondering about first thing in the morning when it was still relatively dark. I remember walking to school one day and thinking that there was a stone in my shoe and stopping to take it out, only to discover it was a 'clock' that had crawled into my shoe. I still get shivers when I think of it. This house was to be our home for the next ten years until we moved to the outskirts of Belfast when a third child, my second brother came along.

Apart from the cockroaches, I have many fond memories of living in Coolbeg Street. I remember, playing football in the street; climbing and swinging on the

WINDSOR

Donegall Road Belfast

PHONE 28013

Coming Attractions

Continuous Performance
from **6** p.m.

Matinee Monday, Wednesday
and Saturday at **3** p.m.

ADMISSION:
Balcony, 1/- Stalls, 6d and 4d
MATINEE, 6d and 3d

FREE CAR PARK.

Windsor Cinema

gas street lights; playing 'rap the doors', much to the annoyance of the neighbours; and making 'guiders' from old pram wheels and bits of wood. Behind the first row of houses there was an 'entry' that ran alongside a high stone wall which separated the entry and houses from the City Hospital. In it was a grassy bank where we played soldiers and could fall down without fear of injury when you were 'shot dead.' One major rule always was, "you couldn't hit a moving target," and so everybody would run around like mad things and shoot their imaginary guns. It was hectic but great innocent fun.

Fridays and Saturdays were sort of special. Friday was 'pay day' when dad would usually give me a sixpence. I'd go to our local 'chippy' on the Donegal Road with three friends and together we would pool our money and buy one plate of chips between us with four forks. I think that is where I learnt to eat quickly, because if you took it easy the chips

Ulster Museum

would rapidly disappear before you had had your proper share. On Saturdays, if the money was available, I would go to the Windsor Picture House (cinema) on the upper Donegal Road opposite Richview Presbyterian Church, usually to watch a western. If there was no money (that was a frequent occurrence) I'd visit the Ulster Museum, where entry was free. My favourite thing was to go and view Takabuti, the Egyptian mummy. I remember being simultaneously fascinated and frightened by her. After that I'd go with friends and play for hours in the Botanic Gardens, making sure I'd visit the Palm House and the Tropical Ravine, where I was sure wild animals lived. Although usually away from home for hours on end my parents never seemed to worry where I was. Changed days now, I fear.

At the time I didn't realise that we were relatively poor until I saw some old photographs of me and my two younger brothers sitting on items we had collected for the annual street bonfire. We were dirty, not exactly dressed to impress and looked a bit like orphaned tramps. However, we were

Tropical Ravine in Botanic Gardens Belfast

smiling and obviously happy and unaware of our circumstances. Maybe being poor is why my mum used to send me to the local bakery/cake shop on a regular basis to ask if they had any 'broken biscuits' or why we were frequent visitors to the pawn shop in Donegal Pass. I certainly knew that 'getting things on tick' was

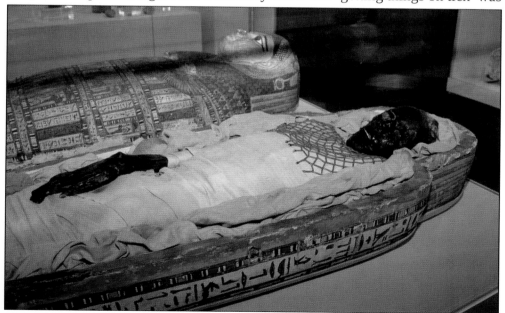

The mummy of Takibuti

a regular occurrence, even though at the time I didn't quite know what this meant. Regardless, poor or not, I was happy.

It was during my time in Coolbeg Street that I first started to learn about God. Richview Presbyterian church halls were at the corner of Coolbeg Street and the Donegal Road, so I joined the church's "Life Boys" and attended Sunday School every week to have my 'card stamped'. Here I learnt the catechism, had memory verses and portions of scripture to learn, as well as hearing bible stories. During the week I went to a children's meeting in a local Belfast City Mission hall. There we sang choruses, heard bible stories and were regularly asked if we 'wanted to be saved'. Many times I responded, not because I really knew what I was doing or felt God call me, but because those who did respond were allowed to select a book to take home and keep from a great pile stored in a small room at the back of the hall. Looking back, I am sure God saw my raised hand and planted a seed within me which was to germinate many years later. I do remember that as a child, when I swore or cursed, something inside me made me repeat the words "God forgive me". Each time I really meant it, so I must have had an inner belief and fear of God.

In addition to these formal settings, during good weather a man would appear in our street ringing a bell. He was armed with a 'flannel graph' (high tech in those days) and a blanket and invited children to come and sit and listen to bible stories. Like the other children in the street, I gladly sat on the blanket many times and listened to the bible stories he told and animated on the flannel graph. With all this going on I have no doubt that God was preparing me and building an inner scriptural foundation which I would draw upon in later years.

Primitive St Methodist church on the Donegal Road

On top of all this 'religious' activity, my dad used to take me to Primitive Street Methodist church on Sunday mornings. It was near the bottom of the Donegal Road, just above Sandy Row and the Clock Bar. I can still remember walking hand in hand with him down the Donegal Road, past the library, to the little church. I have only one vivid recollection of what went on inside and I believe it was this that later changed my life. One Sunday morning, when I was about eight years of age, I was sitting looking at and listening to the minister in the pulpit (I think it was the Reverend Norman Taggart). As I sat, watching and listening, I was transfixed and suddenly said into myself that, "I wanted to do that." I wanted to preach. At that point I believe

Me plus my brothers Bill & Colin on bonfire material

God heard me and purposed to make it a reality. However, it would be many years later before this would actually happen.

With the birth of my youngest brother Colin in 1962, our family moved to a new housing development (Suffolk) on the outskirts of West Belfast. To be honest, I felt it was so far away that it might as well have been in a different country. Our

new house, 77 Horn Drive, had three bedrooms (the box room was allocated specifically to me), an inside bathroom with hot running water (a luxury), a living room and a separate kitchen/dinette. The house even boasted a front and back garden, plus a brick built shed at the rear. This was to be my home for the next thirteen years until I got married in August of 1973 and was allocated a two bedroom flat within the Suffolk Housing Estate, not far from my parents.

Because the estate was new and in the early stages of development, those early days in Suffolk were great and exciting. Friends were easily made, as

Me and my brother Bill outside our new home in Suffolk

11

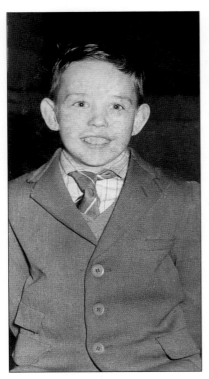
Hugh Dressed for church

everybody was new to the area. There was much to explore and many green spaces to play in, especially along the banks of the Colin Glen river which ran parallel to Suffolk Road. One of the favourite things my friends and I used to do was to take, or to be more accurate, steal, ropes from the Colin Glen pig factory and construct rope bridges across the river. Invariably this frequently meant sodden socks and shoes, usually resulting in a 'telling off' from mum. But it was well worth it. Suffolk was a far cry from Coolbeg Street in Belfast where I used to play, but much, much more exciting.

I am not sure how it came about, but soon after we had moved to Suffolk, my dad, together with a few other men, who I assume were Methodists, were instrumental in getting a Methodist church started in Suffolk. The church was called 'Upper Falls (Suffolk) Methodist' and became part of the Finaghy and Seymour Hill circuit. This was under the guidance of the Reverend Walter Bingham, who was the superintendent minister stationed at Finaghy.

Initially an old school building, basically consisting of two large and one small room, was purchased for use as our church. This, although rough and ready and heated only by open fireplaces, was to act as our church premises for a number of years. I have many fond memories of this building, probably because as a young boy I was seeing it through 'rose tinted glasses.' To me there was a warmth and genuine friendliness about the people who attended the church. Although my dad was a very active member, my mum wasn't overly interested and attended only on an infrequent basis. I can only assume my dad was a Christian, but I don't know how or when this came about.

Whether it was because my father was deeply involved in church life, or because I was drawn into it, I became deeply involved as well, even though I was probably only aged twelve or thirteen. I attended church services twice on

Sunday, many times helping to give out the hymn books as people arrived for the services. In spite of my young age I used to tramp the streets of Suffolk every Friday evening, collecting money for the church building fund, as, with a growing congregation, we were rapidly outgrowing our old school building and needed more space.

I had joined the cub pack and later the Scout Group and went to Sunday School each Sunday afternoon. Then, when someone heard me singing and thought I had a good voice, I was drafted into the church choir and attended the weekly choir practice. My one big recollection of choir in those early days was singing a solo, Away in a Manger, at a Christmas carol service. I was probably eleven or twelve years of age at most. The sight of the Christmas tree and the blazing fire are etched into my memory, as well as me standing like a lost soul in front of the church, hoping I wouldn't make any mistakes as I sang my way through the verses. However, even with all this church activity around me, God was not really in my thinking. Church and its associated activities, was mainly a social outlet that gave me a sense of belonging.

I can't recall when or why it happened, but during my mid-teens I completely rebelled against God. I stopped attending church and dropped out of all the activities that I had been involved in. Instead, I used to go to youth groups in other churches and actively speak against God, His commandments and the way Christians were meant to behave and live. I would purposely make a point of disagreeing and arguing with the leaders of these groups. I suppose one saving grace was that I never said that God didn't exist or wasn't real.

I was on a downward path. I started working at aged seventeen, in Gallaher's Research & Development Division, which was based in Belfast, and this led to roughly a five year period of heavy drinking and gambling. My behaviour broke my parents' hearts, causing my father to strike me one evening after I had

Nora Bradford & Beryl Hanvey in Suffolk church.

come home drunk after yet another drinking session. It was the first and only time that I ever remember my dad striking me and probably was evidence that he had had enough and was at a loss as to what to do. At the time it didn't really bother me, but I still bear an inner scar and am still ashamed and saddened at the way I treated my parents all those years ago.

In those dark days I seemed powerless to break the cycle and, in many ways, can now identify with the way the prodigal son treated his father. My language had also become terrible, filled with swear words and obscenities. I was a mess. Looking back now I am sure my dad must have been fearful about my future, given that his dad, my grandfather, had turned to drink and most likely, as a consequence of this, lost a highly successful business.

At rock bottom, two things happened which led to a complete turn-around in my life. The first was an instantaneous change. I was walking through Belfast, on Great Victoria Street, near the gates of the Royal Belfast Academical Institute when, out of the blue, something in my head said to me that my language was terrible and needed to change. I suddenly felt ashamed and convicted, realizing the truth of this. At that moment I decided that I would stop swearing and cursing and take control of my language. I did this and have continued to do so ever since. I can only put it down to God, through the Holy Spirit, convicting and touching me, beginning a process of bringing me back to Him. Little did I know then that God would use me to speak forth His word to bring encouragement, comfort and hope to His people in years to come. I acquaint this event with the time God, through an angel, touched the lips of Isaiah when he felt his lips (i.e. his language) were unclean and that he was totally unworthy of seeing God (Isaiah 6 verses 5 – 8).

The second thing that happened is quite amusing. My brother Bill, who is 5 years younger than me, used to go to the church youth club held in the old school building. One evening while there, he got into a dispute over table tennis with an older girl and was so annoyed that he came home. I happened to be at home at the time, so he asked if I would come with him to the church youth club and 'sort out' the girl who had annoyed him. Having nothing better to do I agreed and went with him. When we entered the building, he pointed the girl out, her name was Hilary Coard, and said to her, "You're in trouble now."

I promptly walked over to the girl and asked if I could take her home, much to the annoyance of my brother. She agreed and later that evening I walked her to her home in the Finaghy Housing estate, about 2 miles away, being chaperoned at a distance by two of the men who helped run the youth club, Joe Mawhinney and Brian Quinn. This initial "date" over time led to romance, engagement and ultimately marriage. As I write this, Hilary and I have now been married almost fifty years. Meeting Hilary, and forging a loving relationship with her, opened a doorway for me to, re-enter church; combat and overcome my heavy drinking and gambling; and restore a good relationship with my mum and dad. I firmly believe that God had a plan to bring us together so that He could continue His work to refine and shape me.

Although Hilary lived in Finaghy, she attended the Methodist church in Suffolk that my family belonged to and that my dad had helped get started. Over time, no doubt due to Hilary's influence, I reconnected with the church, ending up in the choir, singing alongside Hilary and my mum, who had since committed her life to Jesus through the ministry of the Reverend Jack Robinson. It didn't occur to me that "I wasn't saved" even though Hilary and I attended church on a regular basis and heard the gospel message time and time again.

Hilary and my wedding day

In August 1973 Hilary and I were married and allocated a flat in the Suffolk housing estate near my parents and the church. This seemed to open flood gates of church activity and involvement. We found ourselves, singing in the choir; taking Sunday school; running the youth club; leading the cub scouts; and helping to run a youth fellowship, which met in our flat on Sunday evenings. Yet, in spite of hearing the gospel Sunday by Sunday, being swamped in church activity and having a firm grounding in the bible due to my childhood's religious education, I had never committed myself to Jesus. I wasn't saved. What a hypocrite. I was teaching young people in the fellowship meetings that they had to be saved, but I wasn't. However, that was about to change.

SALVATION AND ENTRY INTO THE PULPIT WITHIN METHODISM

B y the mid 1970's Hilary and I were core church members, but still unsaved. The old school premises had been replaced with a modern church building, which had been built on the same site. Although it was during the Troubles and the church was in the middle of West Belfast, not far from the Woodburn army base and police station, it still had a good congregation and was very active and full of life. Unfortunately, as the Troubles escalated the church had to close some years later. The main building is still there but now houses an Undertakers. It is sad to consider this given the vibrancy and vitality that had made the church so alive in times past.

During a series of Holy Week services during Easter 1975, taken by the Reverend Jack Robinson, I began to feel uncomfortable about my spiritual life and my relationship (or rather lack of it) with God. I tried to shake this of and come that Saturday I felt that I had.

However, during the Easter Sunday services the uneasiness returned. I felt at a loss as to what to do… so I did nothing. Later that evening Hilary and I, as usual, hosted the youth fellowship meeting in our home. At the close of the meeting, after all the young people had left, our friend Jack Hanvey, who had been instrumental in getting us to open up our home for the youth fellowship, turned to us as he was leaving and said, "Don't you think it's time you caught yourselves on?"

I knew exactly what he meant and immediately said, "Yes". In the moments that followed, Hilary and I bowed together on our sofa and committed our lives to Jesus. At the time I felt that a burden had been removed, I felt 'clean', renewed and strangely happy. I went to bed at peace but wondering how I would feel in the morning. I need not have worried, for in the morning I still felt at peace, happy and, more importantly, 'saved.'

Because it was Easter Monday, Hilary and I were on holiday. After getting ready and having breakfast we went to see my mum to tell her our news. When we entered the house she looked at us and knew there was something different about us. She was overjoyed when we told her what had happened the previous evening. She told us that she had been praying for it for quite a while. God bless mothers. I can't recall how it came about, but soon after telling mum we met our minister, Jack Robinson. My mum kept saying, "Tell him." So, I explained that we had become Christians the previous night. He was really shocked and taken aback, but delighted, as he thought that we were already Christians because of our deep involvement in the church.

As an aside, I have to say that going to church and being involved in religious activities does not bring salvation. Accepting Jesus is the only way. It is easy to fool people with all the external stuff as I had done, but God can't be fooled.

I quickly developed a real hunger for scripture, reading and studying the bible at every opportunity. Early on I remember reading the story of where Solomon had a dream in which God asked him what he wanted (1 Kings 3) and Solomon replied, wisdom. This pleased God, so He gave him wisdom but riches as well. I

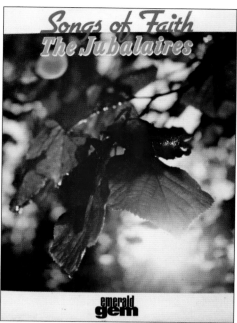

immediately felt led to pray that God would give me wisdom to understand and speak out His word. I believe God heard me, like He did when I was a young boy in Primitive Street Methodist church and, over the years, allowed me to find life in His word for others as well as myself. I developed a real desire to spread the gospel and wanted to do all I could to share God's word.

Initially this led me to form a group that consisted mainly of Hilary and the Reverend Jack Robinson's three children, Michael, Caroline and Gillian. We went anywhere we could get an invite, singing, giving testimony and sharing the gospel. A few times I travelled with a Gospel Group called the Jubilaires that Jack Hanvey played bass guitar for. I used to share the gospel after they had sung. This was great platform and experience for what was to come.

I am not exactly sure how or when it came about but eventually I found myself going out to speak at or take meetings on my own. I need to say that my wife Hilary always went with me, to offer support and has continued to do so from then until now. One regular 'customer' in those early days was my uncle, Eddie Curliss. After becoming a Christian, from a 'rocky' and 'colourful' background, he became the pastor of Lord Street Belfast City Mission Hall before becoming a minister in the Church of the Nazarene and then later a Methodist minister,

Lord Street

ending up in ministering in Scotland. Looking back to those early days in Lord Street, I am sure Eddie just wanted me to come and share my testimony, but I would usually get carried away and end up preaching. To his credit he never complained.

The experience of preaching and the way it made me feel alive, coupled with my desire to do more for God, prompted me to apply to become a lay/local preacher within the Methodist church. This led to a period of tutoring by the Reverend James McCormack during 1977/78. The tutoring took place in his vestry within Seymour Hill Methodist Church. The topics of study were, Homiletics (how to put a service together and conduct one's self in the pulpit); the Sermons of Charles Wesley; and the Old and New Testaments. All my learning was to be assessed through a written examination and in a trial service conducted in Finaghy Methodist church sometime during 1978. I remember that I preached on the "I Am's of Jesus". Shortly after this service I found out that I had passed and duly became a fully accredited local preacher. This opened up new doors for me as a preacher and led to many opportunities to 'take to the pulpit' on the local church circuit. It is my strong belief that God opened this doorway for me, given that Jesus is 'The Door.'

For the next number of years, I was able to preach, on a fairly regular basis, in the following Methodist churches, Upper Falls Suffolk (my home church); Seymour Hill; Finaghy; Jennymount; and Sandy Row (incidentally the church where my grandparents on my dad's side were married). One big regret is that I never got to preach in Primitive Street Methodist church where I first declared

20

inwardly that I wanted to be a preacher. By the time I had become a lay preacher it had long since gone due to redevelopment in the area. Sandy Row Methodist was the closest that I ever got to it.

Many times, in those early days as I preached, I had the very real sense that God was speaking directly and specifically to individuals within the various congregations. Sometimes this was confirmed through people providing positive feedback and/or responding to the message. This is something that has stayed with me through my years of preaching. Many times people have approached me after services to say that God clearly spoke to them through the words that were imparted. In some cases, people have shared about being saved, reconnected with God and even healed of physical or mental ailments. The thought that God knows and cares about individuals and their circumstances continues to excite me and still causes me to seek God for the right words as I prepare sermons.

Seymour Hill Methodist Church

It was during these early days of lay ministry that I was introduced to the Person and work of the Holy Spirit. As I led services and took meetings I had an inner feeling that there was more to the Christian life than what I had been taught and had experienced. Two books, by written by Dennis and Rita Bennett, 'Nine O'Clock in the Morning' and 'The Holy Spirit and You', were given to me by my friend and mentor Jack Hanvey. These proved invaluable and provided many answers to inner questions. They opened up my understanding of the role and work of the Holy Spirit in the Godhead and in the life of individual Christians like me. What I learnt and have since witnessed and experienced would easily take up another book. Suffice to say that The Holy Spirit is a source of knowledge, wisdom, understanding and power who cannot be ignored. It is He who gives insight, boldness and ultimately success within ministry.

One might get the impression that life was easy being a Christian and that all was now working out. This, however, was far from the truth. I like everyone else had and have problems, worries and fears. One major cause of anxiety to me and Hilary in those early days was the fact that we had no children after having tried for a number of years and then being told by experts that we couldn't conceive. It was a constant source of grief and crying out to God in prayer. Then something amazing happened. A couple who had recently returned from Australia started coming to our church in Suffolk. Apart from saying hello we didn't really know them very well and they didn't know us. One day when I was at the work, the lady called to our home to speak to Hilary. She told Hilary that when she had been doing her housework she felt led to pray for us and felt that God had given her a message for us. She said she had put off coming because she was worried as to how she would be received and the doubts she had. She then explained that she felt God instruct her to tell Hilary that she would be pregnant before the end of the year.

Obviously, there were a few teas shed as Hilary told our story to her. God is

Dedication of my daughter Ellen by Rev Jack Robinson

nothing if not faithful however and a few days before the end of that year Hilary indeed discovered that she was pregnant. By then the couple had returned to Australia and we never heard from them again or were able to relay our news. Isn't it amazing how God uses people? The next year, slightly premature on 31 July, our daughter Ellen was born. We look upon her as our miracle. Who says that God doesn't know us or care?

Two years later Hilary discovered that she was pregnant again. We were filled with joy, but sadly this wouldn't last. At about eight months into her pregnancy Hilary went into labour and so we headed off to the Royal Victoria Hospital. However, in the hospital, the medical team thought the baby was coming too early and so gave Hilary an experimental drug to stop her labour. The drug did its job and we were told to go home and return in a week's time for an assessment of how things were. However, during this week the baby died and Hilary ended up having to deliver an almost full term stillborn baby. It was a baby girl who we called Susan. Needless to say we were both devastated and shed many tears. Again, I discovered that being a Christian isn't all sunshine and roses. God never promised that, but He did however promise to be with us in the bad as well as the good times and to bring good out of bad, something I can honestly testify about.

Because of our grief we let the hospital attend to our baby and its burial. But as the years went by this is something that I deeply regretted and blamed myself for. I didn't know if or where our baby was buried. I also blamed the medical team for our baby's death and carried deep rooted unforgiveness against them for decades until God stepped in. Some thirty odd years after Susan's death, after a few church moves, a friend in Lisburn Christian Fellowship, Jenny McRoberts, gave me a book called 'The Shack'. She said that she felt led by God to do this and that I needed to read it. It was a book that dealt with forgiveness in a unique way. At the end of reading the book I was convicted and able to speak forgiveness to myself and more importantly to the medical team that I had blamed for the death of our baby. Through this act I gained a sense of peace. I realised that speaking out forgiveness was for my benefit.

Shortly after this I found a little book called 'Singing in the Shadows' in one of our drawers at home. I had never seen it before. This told the story of a Christian woman in Belfast. She like us had had a stillborn baby and had let the hospital look after the remains. However, years later she discovered the hospital had a

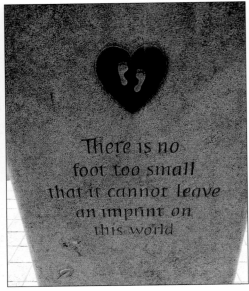

There is no
foot too small
that it cannot leave
an imprint on
this world

burial site in Belfast City Cemetery for babies and was able to find out where her child was buried. This intrigued me and so one day I decided to go to the cemetery and see if there was any information about our baby. To be honest I went in hope rather than expectation, as I didn't expect to find anything. When I enquired in the office about our baby the supervisor went into another room and came back carrying a massive book. I immediately thought of the Lamb's book of life. The man opened it at the date I gave him. To my amazement there

was an entry for Baby McAllister. He gave me a map and directions to the baby plot and where our baby had been buried. I went and got Hilary and together we found the place where our baby girl, Susan, was. We both stood and cried and were later able to put a marker on the spot. Our had been found and a cloud had been lifted from me after over thirty years. I believe God led me on that journey to find peace, after all He is The Way. The circle had been completed when I decided to forgive.

"Forgiving others, although never easy, can give **you** freedom and release and restore a sense of inner peace."

The famous escape artist Harry Houdini

INTO FELLOWSHIP CHURCHES

Over several years within Upper Falls Methodist, and the wider Finaghy church circuit, I found myself in a position of authority and responsibility. I was a recognised lay preacher and as such became a member of the church's leaders' board, helping to make important decisions concerning the life of the church. I ran a weekly home group for church folk who were interested in fostering a deeper relationship with God. Because of my experience of running a youth fellowship I was appointed Circuit Youth Secretary, having responsibility for the non-uniformed youth activities of the circuit's three churches. I felt fulfilled and that I was 'doing something for God'. I am sure there was some inner pride involved. However, there came a point

King's Way Church, formerly Dunmurry Christian Fellowship

where I began to feel constrained and frustrated. I put much of this down to the appointment of a new young minister to lead the church in Suffolk. He, I am sure because he wanted to fulfil his calling, reduced the opportunities of ministry by others in the church, including myself. Looking back, I believe God was shaking me loose and, like many times in the bible, He was changing circumstances so that he could lead me to a new pasture and situation where I could continue my development and growth. So, with some sadness I eventually left the Methodist church, setting aside my church leadership and preaching role and joined Dunmurry Christian Fellowship as an ordinary member. In my head was the thought that, "You don't need a title to minister."

This fellowship church had been started by two friends, Robert Mearns and Ken Brown. Robert, or Bobbie as I knew him, took the leading role, being the more dynamic and charismatic of the two. Ken was content to sit back and play a 'fatherly role,' holding things together. I remember with some amusement the first Sunday Hilary and I went to their service. It was held in a large room above shops on the Lisburn Road. I went dressed in a three piece pin stripped suit with shirt and tie. When I looked around I felt like a real 'fish out of water' as everyone else was wearing casual clothes. Somebody actually came up to me laughing and said that I, "looked like a Presbyterian." I didn't make the same mistake again.

This was to be our spiritual home for over 14 years. In those early days I was content to sit in the background and enjoy the spontaneity of the services, the totally different form of worship and the emphasis on personal ministry. I had entered this new church having laid aside my previous church status, not knowing what to expect or if or how God would use me in the future. I was just 'Joe Bloggs.'

I embraced this new church and new experience, learning much about the reality and love of God and seeing God move in wonderful ways to physically heal people and set them free from fears, anxieties and addictions. Hilary and I were quickly accepted by the church community and made many lifelong friends. For many years the church met in rented or borrowed accommodation including the British Legion Hall near Finaghy Crossroads, Friends Meeting House just off the Lisburn Road, premises in Elmwood Avenue where the Ulster Orchestra used to practice, Belfast Bible College and the Beechlawn Hotel, until finally purchasing an old Co-Op building in the middle of Dunmurry, which is still its meeting place today.

As the building was on Kingsway, the church later changed its name to King's Way Church, as this was felt to be prophetic. Over time, without planning it or attempting to gain any status, I found myself again leading a home group and being responsible for many young people who belonged to the church and who had ended up living in Suffolk. It was like Hilary and I were mum and dad to many grown up children. We loved it, although it presented many difficulties and problems. Maybe God was filling the yearning we had always had for more children.

It was during our time in Dunmurry Christian Fellowship that Hilary and I adopted a little boy of twenty months called Andrew. Rather than being the straightforward process we envisaged, it proved to be a frustrating, difficult, fearful and almost heartbreaking experience. It was another dark valley in which we experienced, and needed, God's grace and provision. Looking back now upon the whole episode, God was definitely in charge, although in the midst of things it didn't appear that way.

Firstly, we nearly missed the adoption cut off age. Although we had applied to adopt in my early to mid-thirties, the cut of age for adoptive parents being forty, we had received little or no word concerning the adoption as I approached my crucial fortieth birthday. Getting rather concerned, I made contact with the appropriate department within the DHSS. They very quickly swung into action (my impression was that they had forgotten about us or didn't realise my age) and assigned a student social worker to assess Hilary and I as suitable adoptive parents. Our daughter Ellen was also involved in this process to determine whether she would accept a newcomer into the family. To our delight the outcome of the assessment was positive, and we were deemed fit to adopt. This experience showed me that the assessment process was primarily aimed at ensuring that an adoptive child's best interests were paramount and top priority and would lead to the placement of a child only with stable, secure and loving people who would ensure it was grafted into their family. To me it spoke about us being adopted into God's family and the loving, faithful character of God who has our best interests at heart.

Although deemed fit to adopt there was no guarantee that this would happen. A major stumbling block was the rule that you couldn't adopt a child from the area you were living in. Given that we lived in the greater Belfast area and that it generated the majority of adoption cases, the idea of Social Services finding a

Andrew's First Christmas with us in Ballymena

suitable child for adoption in the tight timeframe looked highly unlikely. Suddenly things changed. Gallaher Ltd, who I worked for within its R&D Division, took the decision to close its Belfast operations and relocate them to its large Ballymena plant. I took the option to relocate our home to Ballymena, thus opening up greater Belfast for an adoption area. Within a short space of time a toddler of twenty months had been identified for us to adopt. God's timing had been perfect. Like the bible says, "God's ways are higher than our ways and His thoughts higher than our thoughts (Isaiah 55 v 9)".

However, this wasn't the end. Andrew's foster carers had been incorrectly told by their social worker that he would never be put up for adoption and so the decision to do this was a great shock to them. They quickly took out an injunction forbidding us to visit their home. This meant that the usual process of regular home visits over a 6 month period, allowing us to get to know Andrew and for him to get to know us, couldn't happen. As a result, Andrew was taken from his foster carers much earlier than planned and handed over to us in Ballymena. He came with one small bag, he still has it, which contained all of his possessions. Rather than being traumatised by the experience, Andrew settled with us almost immediately and very soon became part of the family.

But this still wasn't the end. His foster carers, who were in their late fifties, applied to adopt Andrew. This was rejected due to their age and so they took Social Services to court on the grounds of age discrimination. We ended up having to engage a lawyer and attend the court proceedings. In the end the judge decided that it was in Andrew's best interests to be placed with us for adoption. This was a great relief. In due course this decision was formalised and ratified in court. At the end of the final hearing, Andrew, who was by then about two and a half years old, called out to the judge, "It's finished." The judge responded by saying, "Yes,

it's finished." The adoption process, and journey, was finally over. It brought to mind the words of Jesus on the cross when He declared, "It is finished."

Within the church my confidence grew and due to the freedom and spontaneity within church services, I was able to begin to share God's word from the front, albeit in a different way to my days of preaching within the Methodist church. I became a trusted church member and often experienced God speak clearly and directly through

Andrew with my dad at Lisburn Christmas Tree

me to individuals. God was positioning me yet again. As time passed, much to my surprise, I became the key worship leader within the church. This wasn't because I was a great musician or gifted guitar player, but rather because those around me felt I could 'hear God'. So, I gained a platform as I led worship, allowing me to interject and share during church services what I felt God was saying at a particular point in time. It was a new type of 'pulpit' experience.

During this time I believe I 'grew in God,' learning not just about the gifts of the Holy Spirit but also about the fruit of the Holy Spirit, which is all about character.

Ashley Lodge Fold in Dunmurry

My growth in God must have been recognised because I was appointed to the church leadership team as one of the church elders, helping to oversee the running of the church. Shortly after that I became a trustee of the church (the church had charitable status as it had been set up as a trust) and ended up being responsible for managing the church finances. I was back in a position of authority and responsibility and thought I was settled. However, as usual, God had other ideas.

During and towards the end of 1995 a number of things happened which shook and unsettled me. Firstly, my dad was tragically killed as the result of a road traffic accident. My mum, who was also in the car, was left with serious injuries. Remember when I said that the Christian life wasn't always easy. I was devastated. Hilary and I had to take on the role of looking after my mum, not just until she recovered physically, but long-term involving the running of her household finances and affairs, as my dad had always managed these.

Secondly, changes were happening regarding the church leadership team, as the key leader and co-founder of the Church, Robert Mearns, was planning on moving to the USA. I wasn't happy with the leadership changes that were being proposed and felt uneasy.

Thirdly, Hilary and I, as a result of having our home broken into and our car stolen and burnt out, had decided to move home, from Dunmurry to Lisburn. As a result of all of these factors we ended up leaving Dunmurry Christian Fellowship to look for pastures new within Lisburn. I find it interesting that in Psalm 23 it talks about the shepherd leading sheep to green pastures, plural. God at times moves us on to bring about refreshment with new challenges and opportunities.

Hilary and I were churchless again. As before, when we had left the Methodist church, I had set aside my position and responsibilities. The same thought I had years earlier came back to me, "You don't need a title to minister." The one thing I was actively involved in was running a Sunday evening fellowship for senior citizens in Ashley Lodge Fold, Dunmurry. Basically, I played favourite hymns and choruses on my guitar and shared a short story with a gospel message for those residents who wanted to come along. This fellowship night had come about after an outreach event called, 'Walk of 1000 Men,' which took place in about 1994. I had been asked by my cousin, who was a supervisor in Ashley Lodge Fold at the time, to start up a fellowship meeting. What started off as a short-term commitment turned into a permanent commitment, which only stopped in 2020, as a result of Covid. In running this evening fellowship I learnt that it was church for many who attended and that a pulpit isn't necessarily an elevated ornate wooden structure in a church building. It can simply be a chair and a coffee table.

Due to the success of this Sunday evening fellowship I was asked if I could run something similar in Malone Lodge Residential Home for the residents. I agreed and so, on a monthly basis, my wife Hilary, my mum and I ran a short Sunday morning service. Basically, we led the residents in the singing of well-known hymns, which I accompanied on the guitar, said a prayer and usually shared a short inspirational story. I discovered that having such a pulpit as this was not glamorous and that you needed a sense of humour and a thick skin. On many occasions some of those attending would fall asleep and snore. On one occasion a lady, obviously suffering with dementia, woke up and shouted at me as I was playing the guitar. She was shouting, "Who do you think you are? Why don't you get up off your ass and get a real job?" She was quickly led away by one of the nurses but continued to shout at me to, 'get out,' while making rude gestures with her fingers. What could I do but laugh it off?

These services continued for a number of years until my mum was diagnosed with lung cancer, dying only seven weeks later in our spare bedroom. After this I could never bring myself to return to the residential home as my lasting memory is that of my mum going around the residents handing them out Mission Praise song books and chatting to them.

After leaving Dunmurry Christian Fellowship, we quickly found a new church in Lisburn to attend. This was 'Lisburn Christian Fellowship' (LCF). It was led by George Hilary, ably supported by his wife Melanie, together with a small leadership team. George was the full-time pastor, having given up his career as a solicitor years earlier to lead the church. When we first joined, it met in an old, I think, two room building made as I recall from corrugated iron. In some places there were holes in the floor. It was situated in Wardsborough Road at the rear of Smyth Patterson's department store. Although the building was 'dingy' to say the least, it was very evident that God was there, with people being blessed and touched week by week. Hilary and I quickly discovered the congregation to be caring and warm hearted.

Although Lisburn and Dunmurry Christian Fellowships were similar in many ways, such as their leadership structure, the format of services, including spontaneity and the role of home groups, they also had differences. Looking back now, Dunmurry was more intense and inward looking, focusing on personal ministry. It was competitive in a sense, given that there were many young and very talented people looking to impress the full-time leader, Robert Mearns, who was very charismatic and dynamic. To be honest I probably was one of those looking to impress. On the other hand, Lisburn Christian Fellowship was much less intense, although still being involved in personal ministry. It was also more outward looking, actively supporting missionaries and willing to engage with other churches and Christians regarding outreach. Its focus was mainly on pastoral issues, evangelism and mission. Melanie Hilary had a heart and compassion for struggling people, the 'waifs and strays' and she had a passion for working with children, always striving to build them into the church family. Many times her zeal took the church onto the streets of Lisburn to present the Gospel through music, drama and dance, even balloon shaping. I must confess

Lisburn Christian Fellowship on Queen's Road

having an 'outdoor pulpit' was something I enjoyed.

Although we were usually well received not everybody appreciated what we did. I remember on one occasion when we were having an outreach event in Bow Street, Lisburn, I was 'pulling the crowd in' by saying we had an escapologist who was going to perform and free himself from bonds holding him. So we tied the 'pretend escapologist' up and put him in a sack. Everybody eagerly counted from ten to zero when our fake 'Houdini' was meant to free himself. Of course nothing happened so we gave him some more time with the crowd counting down again. Again, nothing happened as the person continued to wriggle in the sack. I then shouted out, "How do we get him free?" A 'plant' in the crowd then shouted back, "Untie the bonds and loose him." This was my cue to present the Gospel about Jesus freeing us from our bonds of sin. Some of the crowd were furious with us, saying they had been conned. They angrily walked away shouting at us as they went. I can only think that they were Houdini fans.

George on the other hand had heart for mission and was always open to new ideas in terms of church life and its expression of faith. As a result, LCF actively supported a number of overseas ministries and missionaries and organised trips to visit them and for them to visit LCF. In addition, LCF would invite other church leaders, some quite significant ones, to come and hold conferences in our premises, which would be open for anyone to attend. Being open to new ideas George welcomed and supported experimentation in terms of how the church worshipped, prayed and praised God in our services. I should say that he gave prayerful consideration before launching into anything new. This openness

Bow Street, Lisburn

allowed for the use of art, poetry and dance in our services as well as the usual use of music and song. This led to a greater involvement of people in church life and helped folk feel they could contribute. It also helped create a sense of belonging and acceptance.

As my wife Hilary and I became rooted in the church the same cycle of events unfolded as had been the case in Dunmurry. I became a trusted member of the church as my gifting for bringing and sharing God's Word was recognised. I was able to share 'off the cuff' during services when I sensed that God wanted me to say something. George also allowed me to preach in a formal capacity when I felt I had something to share. Over time I became a home group leader and actively supported my wife Hilary when she took over the running of the 'mums and toddlers' group.

As in Dunmurry, I was eventually appointed to the church's leadership team and later became chair of the Trustees. Again, church was fulfilling and satisfying, giving me an outlet for preaching and ministering. As I stated previously, George was very much open to new ideas and creativity, encouraging as well as suggesting, new ways to worship and communicate with and about God. As a consequence our services could be 'different to the norm' depending on how God's Spirit was leading.

One of my highlights in LCF was writing and producing a musical drama called

'Reach for the Throne', which the church put on over two nights to packed audiences. The aim was to present the Gospel in a novel way. The idea for it came about when I first heard Mary Black and Eleanor McEvoy's song 'A Woman's Heart' and in the course of a split second seen in my mind God's dealing with mankind from creation to the return of Jesus. I must say George was very supportive of the whole concept, evidence of his openness for new ideas.

Another real joy was leading a team from LCF to a little church in Sombor, Serbia, which LCF supported, and seeing many people respond to the gospel, some being physically healed. In LCF I found a new freedom of expression and a definite outlet for sharing the Gospel in different ways and places. Pulpit took on a new meaning. However, after having been involved in Lisburn Christian Fellowship for about eighteen years, things were about to change again and go full circle for Hilary and me.

Sombor Town in Serbia

View of Lower Lough Erne from Clareview Leisure Park

BACK TO METHODISM

In the summer of 2014, Hilary and I went to visit friends who were in the process of moving their caravan from the Loan Eden caravan site, situated just outside Kesh in County Fermanagh, to Clareview Country Park. This new site was only a few miles away, overlooking Lower Lough Erne. It had good facilities, beautiful scenery and was very well maintained. In the process of viewing their new pitch at Clareview, as well as the Park in general, we met the site owner, Mervyn Duncan. What a character and what a salesman. Totally out of the blue and totally out of character for me, I ended up buying a caravan! Looking back, I still find this hard to believe, as normally I don't make rash decisions, especially when large sums of money are involved. However, this purchase started off a whole chain of events that over time resulted in Hilary and I leaving LCF and re-joining the Methodist Church after an absence of over thirty years. I truly believe that God was behind it and directing our path.

Pettigo Methodist Church

I feel it important at this point to mention that sometime after we left LCF, Melanie Hilary was diagnosed with cancer. After battling the cancer for quite a

39

while and receiving much treatment, she sadly died in October 2015, leaving George, her family and the church devastated. To many, including me, Melanie had been a central figure in LCF and a significant part of the 'heart' of the church. She was a true woman of God. Although George continued to lead the church after Melanie's death, I feel he was never the same. A few years later George led LCF to join with The Journey Church in Lisburn and sadly LCF no longer exists in its own right.

Something inside me kept saying we had made the right decision about the purchase of the caravan and so I felt at peace. Because, I reckoned, we would be spending a lot of time at the caravan, certainly over summer periods, I sensed it was only right that I talked to George Hilary about stepping out of LCF church leadership. I can't explain it, but the timing seemed right. George and his wife Melanie were very gracious about this and agreed with me that it was the right thing to do. My thinking was that while at home we would continue to attend LCF and when at the caravan we would seek out a local church near Kesh to attend. So, over a period of maybe 3 or 4 weeks Hilary and I drove around the Kesh area trying to find a suitable church. However, for a number of reasons, nothing seemed to work out. Then, rather by accident, or so we thought, we found a Methodist church in Pettigo. This was right on the Fermanagh/Donegal border and only about six miles from our caravan. We duly took note of the time of the Sunday services and decided to attend the following Sunday.

When we arrived the following Sunday we were given a very warm welcome. Although the service was so different to what we were used to in LCF we felt very much at home. As the service unfolded and as I listened to the sermon being preached, I had the same sort of feeling I had as a little boy in Primitive Street Methodist. I felt God was calling me to preach again within the Methodist Church. This feeling remained with me, so much so that when Hilary and I returned to our home in Lisburn, I emailed the Methodist Church in Ireland and told them that I used to be a Methodist local preacher many years previously and asked if it was possible for me to take up preaching again within Methodism. I heard nothing for a long time.

Then one day, out of the blue, I received an email from the person who managed local preaching in Ireland, the Reverend Mervyn Ewing. I was totally surprised to find out he was the minister of Seymour Street Methodist Church, which was only about two miles from my home and that he lived practically around the corner from me. I began to think it wasn't a coincidence. Out of all the ministers in Ireland the man I needed to speak to about my question was nearly on my doorstep. We subsequently met for coffee and I explained my background and desire to preach. I found Mervyn very positive and accepting of me and what I wanted to do. When he told me that, unlike all other churches, the office of an accredited lay/local preacher within the Methodist Church is a lifetime office, provided one belongs to a Methodist church, I knew it had to be of God. Mervyn, instead of getting me to rush forward, suggested that I speak to George Hilary and ask him to provide a reference about me if I still wanted to pursue matters. He also suggested that he, George and I could meet to talk things over.

Soon afterwards, I arranged to meet George for coffee and told him about my meeting with Mervyn and what he had said. George told me that providing a reference was no problem and that he would prepare one and send it to Mervyn. I again explained how I felt and that I believed God had confirmed my feelings about re-entering the Methodist Church to become a local/lay preacher again. He was very understanding and accepting of what I told him. He told me that although he and LCF would sadly miss me, I should pursue what I felt God was saying to me. He also agreed that a joint meeting with Mervyn would be useful. This was therefore undertaken a little while later and rather than being a strain, proved very positive and effectively ended with George 'handing me over' to Mervyn. Around the same time a friend shared a thought with me about 'Latter Day Rain', saying that he felt it applied to me. This seemed very apt, given what was going on. I took it as further confirmation of the move back to Methodism and felt I was being given an opportunity to serve God in my latter years and hopefully reap a harvest of what I had sown over the previous forty plus years.

Given the reference that George provided and the meetings that had taken place, Mervyn said he would trust me concerning my previous accreditation as a local preacher as I couldn't find my original accreditation certificate. He said he would give me an opportunity to preach in Seymour Street so that he could, "assess my theology." This took place during an evening Sunday service, after which Mervyn gave me a 'thumbs up'. My name as a local preacher was duly added to the circuit preaching plan and so opened a doorway for me to preach again within the Methodist Church. As well as the opportunity to preach in Seymour Street, this meant that I could be called upon to preach in the other five Methodist churches on the circuit; Trinity, Broomhedge, Magheragall, Dromore and Priesthill. Things were fitting into place. I must confess that my leaving service in LCF was tinged with sadness. However, I felt that I wasn't walking out of but rather into something.

On Sunday 15th March 2015, Mother's Day, when I got up, I read some scripture from John chapter 1. One verse struck me, 'The Word became flesh and dwelt among us.' To me it spoke of God's continuing trust in us, in mankind. Man has failed God since the beginning in the Garden of Eden and yet He trusted Joseph and Mary with His Son. God trusted prophets with His Word. I felt that God was saying to me, "I trust you with my Word," which was very relevant regarding my desire to preach and the change that was happening.

As I walked to Seymour Street Methodist church for the service I began to talk to God telling Him that I had stepped out in faith but was still uncertain it was the right thing to do. I was asking if I had got it all wrong. I asked for some sort of confirmation. In church, as part of the morning service, a couple did a dramatic reading. The first words that they spoke were from John chapter 1 containing the verse, "The Word became flesh and dwelt among us." It was as if God was shaking me and saying, "Do you believe me now?" It was really encouraging for me. I shared all this with the couple after the service. They were really taken aback that God had spoken through them and were encouraged. It was something new for them. I felt for me it was confirmation of a new beginning and harvest.

Unknown to me, the Reverend Mervyn Ewing had written an affirming letter about me to the Reverend Eleanor Hayden, the Methodist minister in Pettigo, confirming my acceptance as a fully accredited local preacher. In it he suggested that I could perhaps be used by her as a local preacher, given that I had a caravan in Kesh and spent much of the summer at it. Before I knew it Eleanor had me on the preaching plan for Pettigo and Irvinestown and called upon me frequently to take services. During this period, my wife Hilary and I found Eleanor very warm, friendly and accepting. We became good friends with her and her husband Gareth, who looked after a number of churches in County Tyrone. He, as well as Eleanor, called upon me to conduct services.

After being in charge of the Pettigo/Irvinestown circuit, the Reverend Eleanor Hayden was moved to the Omagh Circuit by the Methodist Conference. Here she

Seymour Street Methodist Church

had many more churches to oversee, not just two as before. She was supported by her husband Gareth who, among other duties, looked after the preparation and administration of the Circuit's preaching plan. Eleanor asked if I would be prepared to help on her new circuit. I happily agreed and found more churches added to my growing list of pulpits to preach from. At this point I was on the preaching plan for my home Circuit of Lisburn & Dromore, the Pettigo & Irvinestown Circuit plus the Omagh & Fintona Circuit. I ended up preaching in places across County Tyrone that I had never heard of. The doorway to preaching on a regular basis had certainly opened wide, fulfilling my childhood aspiration. However, it was to open even wider. When I had the feeling that first Sunday morning in Pettigo Methodist Church that I should re-enter the Methodist Church, I never realised the amount of doors and pulpits God would open up for me. Jesus showed me that He really is The Door.

Before I end the story of my journey back into the Methodist Church and the re-entering of Methodist pulpits, there are two more things to add. Firstly, the Reverend Mervyn Ewing, who had initially trusted me as a local preacher, moved from Seymour Street, as the superintendent minister and took over the running of the Dundrum, Newcastle & Downpatrick Circuit on a part time/semi-retired basis. As the Reverend Eleanor Hayden had done, following her move to the Omagh and Fintona circuit, Mervyn asked if I would help out with preaching on his new circuit. Again, I readily agreed getting my name added to another preaching plan and led to me preaching in Newcastle and Dundrum Methodist churches.

Secondly, Eleanor Hayden asked if I would be prepared to help out on the Upper Erne circuit, where a new probationer minister, Daphne Hanna, had recently been appointed. I was very happy to help out as I knew Daphne, given that she had been a member of the Lisburn & Dromore Circuit which I belonged to. This has allowed me to preach in Lisnaskea and Drumady Methodist churches.

I feel in these latter years that God has allowed me to preach much more regularly and certainly in many more places than in my former years. My friend's word about, "Bearing fruit in my latter years," seems to have become a reality. As I sit now at the computer, I can only thank God for all the opportunities He has given me to preach His Word. God has certainly proved to me that He is 'The Way' and 'The Door' and responded to a small boy's desire to preach, creating many opportunities for this to happen. If God can do it for me, He certainly can do it for you. All you have to do is trust Him.

YOUR SALVATION

If my story has touched you, encouraged you or maybe even convicted you and you would like to ask Jesus into your life, then below is a prayer used by Billy Graham when leading sinner's to salvation. To receive Jesus and the gift of salvation He offers, all you have to do is pray it in faith.

Dear Lord Jesus, I know that I am a sinner and I ask for Your forgiveness. I believe that You died for my sins and rose from the dead. I turn from my sins and invite You to come into my heart and life. I want to trust and follow You as my Lord and Saviour. In Your Name I pray. Amen.

Pulpits

Below is a list of those pulpits that I have had the privilege to preach in since returning to the Methodist Church in 2014.

Lagan Valley & South Down Circuit (formally Lisburn and Dromore)

Seymour Street, Dromore, Broomhedge, Priesthill, Magheragall and Trinity Methodist

Pettigo & Irvinestown Circuit

Pettigo and Irvinestown

Omagh & Fintona Circuit

Omagh, Mayne, Drumquin, Togheradoo and Fintona

Newcastle, Dundrum & Downpatrick Circuit (Now incorporated as Donard into the new Lagan Valley & South Down Circuit)

Newcastle and Dundrum

Upper Erne Circuit

Lisnaskea and Drumady

Miscellaneous

Seymour Hill, Mountpottinger and Clabby

THE INSPIRED WORD OF GOD

*What follows is a collection of bite size, or meal size,
reflections on God's Word, depending on one's hunger or appetite at any
point in time. It is hoped that they will challenge, encourage and inspire and
perhaps be used in some measure to help present the Gospel.*

Reflection on Newness in God

Introduction

> *If we are honest, we will acknowledge that at different times in our lives we have experienced hardship and distress due to difficulties arising from the likes of, illness and poor health; relationship problems; employment and financial worries; and bereavement. Maybe, like me, at some point you have felt, "I wish I could start again." The good news is that in God there is newness and therefore hope for the future.*

What we Face is Not New

The people mentioned in the bible were no different to us. They also experienced difficulty and hardship and at times struggled to make sense of what was happening to them and around them. Jeremiah, who was a prophet of God, is one example. He wrote the Book of Lamentations as a result of the misery felt by the exiles who were carried off by their Babylonian captors, saddened by the ruin and destruction of their holy city Jerusalem and the persecution that they encountered, and he personally faced as a prophet of God.

In Lamentations he mentions many things that he and his people were experiencing, so much so that He felt God had abandoned them and him. He talked of, physical ailment ; mental and emotional instability; uncertainty; sadness and despair; a lack of peace; and a loss of prosperity. All the sort of things we encounter day to day and have probably experienced in our lives.

Yet, in the midst of his despair, Jeremiah remembered the reality of God. He remembered that God's grace and mercy could be experienced every day and that God was a source of hope for the future. The same holds true for us. God is all about newness, for He said through the prophet Isaiah (43 v 18/19) "Behold I do a new thing; now it shall spring forth; shall you not know it?" We may not be able to change the past, but God can give a better future. If you need newness in your life, turning to God is the key. So, what new things can we receive?

A New Birth and a New Start

When Nicodemus came to Jesus to talk about spiritual matters, Jesus told him that he, "needed to be born again," a phrase well used within church settings and one that was boldly written on the wall above the pulpit in Primitive Street Methodist church where my journey to become a preacher began. However, Nicodemus, who was very well educated in religious matters, didn't understand what Jesus meant. You see being religious doesn't mean we fully understand or comprehend what the Gospel message is all about. It is about relationship not religion. For Nicodemus, Jesus had to spell it out and even then, it is unclear 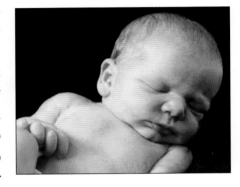 whether he actually understood. Jesus was taking about a spiritual birth, a spiritual awaking to the things of God through Jesus. Saint Paul in his second letter to the church at Corinth referred to this as becoming a new creation, a new person and beginning life afresh. A life in which all past sins are forgiven and forgotten by God. Psalm 103 v 12 endorses this, stating that, "as far as the east is from the west, so far has God removed our transgressions from us." In this new life we start off with a clean slate, we feel clean and at peace and able to approach God because of His grace and mercy. It happens the moment we accept Jesus into our lives as Saviour, believing that He died for our sins and rose from the dead to give new life.

However, we need to know that becoming a Christian isn't a recipe for an easy sin free life. We can still experience temptation, hard times, difficulties and at times get it wrong and fall into sin. Because of this we can feel guilty, ashamed and unable to approach God. The good news, as we read in Lamentations chapter 3 verses 21 – 24, is that God can give us a new start every day. Jeremiah declares that God's mercies are new every morning. Jesus died for all sin, at all time and for all people. This means we can benefit from God's mercy and grace every time we sin if we turn to Him and repent. Everyday can be a new day and a fresh start in Jesus.

A New Heart and New Attitude

The prophet Ezekiel, in chapter 36 verse 26, records the word of God when He declares to His people, "A new heart also will I give you, and a new spirit will I put within you: and I will take away the stony heart and give you a heart of flesh." God knows at times we need an emotional heart transplant. The big question is, "Why?" I believe there are a number of reasons.

We can sustain a broken heart and heartache due to traumatic things which happen in our lives like relationship breakdowns and bereavement. Sometimes the pain won't go away and affects our everyday lives. It may therefore be difficult to trust people again, or maybe feel it's wrong to be happy and enjoy life again. However, according to Isaiah 61, Jesus is about healing the broken hearted. God mends broken hearts.

We can lose heart at times. Sometimes the words and actions of others can affect our self-confidence, causing a loss of enthusiasm and motivation. Our feeling of self-worth can be diminished, causing us to just give up. However, scripture tells us that we have been chosen (1 Peter 2 v 9) and are a treasure and special in Jesus. He reinvigorates us.

We can lose feeling. Our heart can grow cold so that our compassion for others

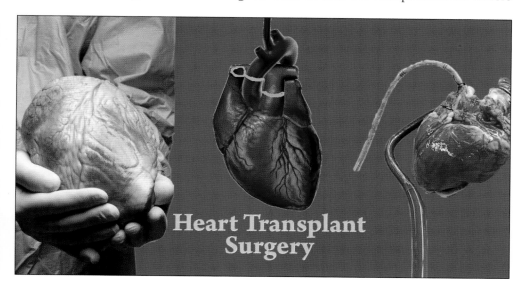

Heart Transplant Surgery

decreases. We reach a point where we are immune to the needs of others. We don't feel the same level of emotion as we did in the past at others pain. Jesus gives new life and feeling so that our compassion is restored.

We can lose our love and passion for God. In Revelation Saint John records God's word for the church, 'You have lost your first love.' Ezekial also says that God puts a new spirit in us. A spirit of desire for God so that we want to read, pray and study and then the courage to share God with others.

A New Future

In the book of Revelation (chapter 21 v 1 – 5), Saint John talks about the vision God gave him. He speaks about a new heaven and a new earth. He speaks about no more sea (a barrier to people coming together), no more tears or death or sadness. Although these words relate to end times, when God's Kingdom will come to earth, I believe it can also speak to us about a new future in Christ, not just beyond death but during life. When asked by the Pharisees, "When would the kingdom of God come?" Jesus said that the Kingdom of God is within you (Luke 17 v 20/21). Therefore God's kingdom which brings about change is already here. Today, God can change the path we are on. He can present new opportunities. He can open closed doors and close open doors. He is concerned with your future, your employment, your education, your relationships and your wellbeing. If you feel trapped or disillusioned with your life, God can intervene and change your outlook and destiny. It is He who holds the key to the future, not luck, chance or astrology.

God can allow you to experience happiness and joy again after hard times, after disappointment, after heartache. He gives the oil of gladness instead of mourning.

Today God calls out afresh, "Behold I make all things, not some things, but all things." It doesn't matter what element of your life needs newness, God can move in and bring about needed change.

Reflection on 'Cross Over'

Introduction

The phrase 'Cross Over' jumped into my mind when I read the account of Jesus dying on the cross and, in particular, the verse when He cried out "It is finished." For Jesus, crying out, "It is finished," meant that His death on the cross and His sacrifice was over. However, I feel it also signified so much more. Let me explain...

Cross Over from Heaven to Earth

In the Gospel of John, chapter 1, it tells us that Jesus was with God, and was God, in the beginning and that northing was made without Him. He dwelt in heaven, having all power and authority. He was worshipped and praised. Yet Jesus decided to 'cross over' from His world into our world. The big question is why?

The answer is given in John 3 v 16 which says, "For God so loved the world that He gave His only begotten son that whosoever believes in Him should not perish but have eternal life." It was out of love that Jesus crossed over. He crossed over from a spiritual realm into physical realm, from a place of holiness into a world of sin, from a place where he was worshipped into a place where he was rejected, from a place of no sickness or pain into a world of problems and hardship and from a place of security into a place of vulnerability.

He did this voluntarily because he loved you, and still does, totally believing that you were worth it. This first 'cross over' started a chain of events which should bring comfort and hope.

Cross Over as The Remedy

When Jesus called out, "It is finished," (recorded in John 19 v 30) He was signifying was that the cross was over. God's remedy for sin, which has been woven all throughout history and scripture, had been finally accomplished. God's word as revealed through the prophets and psalmists in scriptures, such as Isiah 53 and Psalms 22, concerning Christ's suffering and death had been fulfilled. Through the cross Jesus paid the price for all sin, for all time, for all people, including yours and mine. He became the spotless sacrificial lamb as declared by John the Baptist. Scripture says, 'cursed are those that hang on a tree,' and talks about Jesus, 'enduring the shame of the cross. '

When Jesus died on the cross he not only dealt with sin but also its consequences, the shame, the guilt and the fear that we can feel. Through Him we are declared innocent and righteous. As such, there is no longer any need for sacrifices or punishment to deal with sin. St Paul in Romans 5 v 18 tells us, "Just as the result of one sin was condemnation for all men, so also the result of one act of righteousness was justification that brings life to all men." The cross is over, the sacrifice made and the remedy given.

Cross Over as anger has disappeared

Christ's death on the cross dealt with God's need for atonement for sin and made a way for mankind to come to God, to cross over to Him because He wants to receive us. In Hebrews 10 it says we can have confidence to enter the most Holy place, the place where God dwells, because of the blood of Jesus. It goes on to say that Jesus is the new and living way; therefore, draw near to God with a sincere heart in full assurance of faith. If we accept and believe in Jesus and what he accomplished, God is no longer angry or cross with us. The cross face is over.

Instead, it is God's desire to adopt us into His family and be our Father. He wants us to enjoy a new life in Him without fear.

However, it would be remiss to move on without saying that although John 3 v 16 highlights God's love and grace, it also contains a warning. Those who fail to believe and accept Jesus will perish. God will remain cross. His anger is only turned away through our faith in Jesus

Cross Over as a Bridge

Jesus through His obedience to God and His ultimate sacrifice of dying on the cross for all sin made a way for us to come to God. Jesus declared, "I am the way the truth and the life, no man comes to the father but by me." However, salvation doesn't happen automatically because you attend church, belong to a Christian organisation or mingle with Christians. It only comes when there is a definite decision and response to actually cross over into God's Kingdom. It is no good wanting to cross the road, seeing the green man lighting up and just staying put. You have to cross over. With salvation you have to respond to God's initiative and take the steps needed to cross over. You need to confess you are a sinner, ask for forgiveness through exercising faith in Christ's atonement and then thank God in faith for your salvation. Peter tells us in 1 Peter 2 v 9 that because of Jesus, "We cross over from darkness into His marvellous light."

Cross Over our heads

If we accept Christ and come to God by faith, we find not only salvation and acceptance as sons and daughters, but we live under God's protection. We live under the cross. We discover God is really our shelter, our rock, our defender, our shield and our protector, as so many in the bible discovered. The psalms are littered with such descriptors of God. In God the cross is always over us as we live out our lives. We will never be left on our own or abandoned by Him. The Holy Spirit is ever present. And because we live under the cross we can receive and enjoy so much more in God than just His protection. We can discover His real love for us, which can manifest itself in comfort in hard times. We can know strength in times of weakness. We can know His leading and direction in times of feeling lost. We can know His instruction and teaching in times of confusion. We can know His power and deliverance when we feel trapped. No wonder David declared in Psalm 34 v 11 that, "His praise shall continually be in my mouth." We have a God worth praising and unending in His goodness towards us.

Cross Over as reaching Out

In response to a lawyer's question, Jesus talked about loving our neighbours and used the parable of the Good Samaritan to illustrate the point. This leads to our final reflection on 'Cross Over'. Jesus through this parable was making the point that we are meant to cross over in order to reach and provide help to our neighbours, e.g. those around us who are in need. The Samaritan crossed many boundaries to provide aid, such as religion, tradition, enmity, culture, fear of being misunderstood

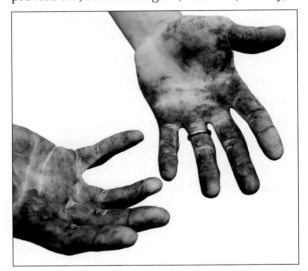

and rejection. These are the sort of boundaries we may have to cross in order to help someone in need. Sometimes it is not enough to pray, there is a need to get our hands dirty and meet a cost to offer practical help, show friendship, give comfort and forgiveness. Being a Christian is not about being passive but about being active. Christianity isn't about living in a bubble or being selfish with what God has given us. God expects us to share His love with others and to cross over to others no matter what the barriers may be. The Samaritan crossed over, overcoming many barriers. Jesus says to us, "Go and do likewise," and Cross Over.

Reflection on God The Rock

If you have ever driven down the Ard's Peninsula from Newtownards to Portaferry, you may have noticed a massive rock (Butterlump Stone) on the foreshore near Greyabbey. I first seen it as a young boy, when in my father's car, as we drove along the road on a day's outing. The memory of it has stayed with me, especially as two teenagers were sitting on top of it and I wished I could climb up it too. When I think of it, I am reminded that God is often described as a rock in the bible, and The Rock,

according to Deuteronomy 32 v 4. God is someone we can sit upon and stand upon because He is steadfast and sure. What follows are my reflections on God the Rock.

God as a Rock of Offence

In 1 Peter 2 v 8 God/Jesus is referred to as a Rock of Offence and a Stone of Stumbling. At first sight this is confusing, if not off-putting, and begs the question why? When Jesus was on earth He didn't mince His words. He called a spade a spade. He always spoke the truth and in doing so offended people, primarily the religious leaders of His day. Jesus called them hypocrites because they weighed the people down with laws, with rules and regulations, but had no real heart for or understanding of God themselves. Jesus spoke about forgiveness and offended those who wouldn't forgive. He spoke of His death and offended His disciples. He spoke about giving to the poor and offended the rich. He spoke against judging others and offended the gossips and accusers. He spoke about loving others and offended the loveless and selfish. He spoke about salvation through Himself and offended the self-righteous.

Jesus is the Word of God and what He said still stands today and still offends those who oppose God. The bible contains God's word, but because it sometimes doesn't fit with people's views or thinking they find it offensive and try to dilute it. But God asks us to embrace and believe His Word and the Gospel so that we will not be offended by it but rather encouraged by it. Is His word offensive to you?

God as a Rock of Salvation

David in Psalm 62 v 1 describes God as his rock and his salvation. Scripture is perfectly clear that salvation is only attainable by grace, through faith in Jesus. It can't be won, earned, or bought (Ephesians 2 v 8). This is an unchanging and constant fact. Salvation is like a large unmovable rock that can be depended upon, rested upon and believed in. It gives us hope and saves us from the consequences of sin which are fear, guilt, shame and ultimately God's judgement. God wants our salvation to be sure and permanent and hence He offers forgiveness and mercy all throughout life. God is unchanging and His mercy and forgiveness are never ending. When we sin and get it wrong the truth is we can come to God because of what Jesus did through the cross and find

renewal and acceptance. We can climb upon the rock again and find rest and peace. Because God's mercies are new every morning (Lamentations 3 v 22/23) we can find and experience renewal every day.

In the book of Revelation (2 v 17) it talks about the victorious, those Christians who ran the race and stayed true, receiving a white stone or piece of rock to symbolise innocence, election and acceptance into God's kingdom. Depend on The Rock as your salvation.

God as a Rock of Foundation

Saint Peter, in his first letter, describes Jesus as the chief corner stone – or a rock of foundation. God wants us to be secure as we grow and live out our lives. As Christians, we are meant to mature and develop, exhibiting the fruit of the Holy Spirit which Paul talks about in Galations chapter 5. That's why God has provided guidelines in scripture to help us in every area of our lives, whether spiritual or natural. That's why Jesus came as the Word of God, to make things plain and understandable. Jesus was The Word that became flesh and dwelt among us, to reveal and explain scripture and reveal God's plan for mankind. That's why Jesus sent His Holy Spirit to guide us, teach us and lead into truth so that we would be secure in our walk with God. The foundational truths and guidelines, as taught by Jesus and found in scripture, still apply today to our spiritual lives, instructing us in terms of honouring God, how to pray, the need to forgive and the value of the scripture etc.

They also show us how to treat others: husbands, wives, children, parents, employees, employers and neighbours, so we can know peace. God's foundation is fixed and doesn't change. If you build your life around God, and upon God the Rock, you will find and know security. Be like the man who built his house on the rock which stood firm in the storms of life.

Building on the Rock

God as a Rock of Strength and Refuge

David in Psalms 62 and 94 declared that God was his mighty rock and rock of refuge and asked people to trust in God at all times. I am sure because of the difficulties and hardships he encountered during his life, even as a king, he could say this with confidence from real experience. No matter what status we may have or what position we may hold, or how financially secure we are, the truth is at times we all encounter hardship and difficulties. I know all about this. All of us at times feel weak and lack confidence to do certain things. It may be praying out loud in church, testifying, reading or taking Sunday school. It could be to do with relationships or maybe employment. Sometimes we suffer temptation and our faith is tested. But the good news is that God equips us and strengthens us in times of weakness and helps us to overcome, by restoring our self-confidence, giving us courage and helping us to be bold.

Paul knew all about this and said, "God's strength is made perfect in our weakness." Even the act of forgiving at times needs strength, for the bible talks about, 'the power to forgive.' Just know the strength of God is available to all who believe in Him. But as well as providing strength in times of weakness, God is also a rock of refuge. He is someone to go to when there is a need to find comfort and just be at peace for a while. God won't turn away those who need Him, but rather will embrace those in need. Jesus calls out, "Come unto me all you who are weary and heavy laden and I will give you rest." Sometimes it's not strength we need, it's just a shoulder to cry on, someone to lend a listening ear and somewhere to rest. Why not try God?

God as a Rock of Victory

In the book of Daniel (chapter 2) the prophet interprets the dream that the king Nebuchadnezzar had. This was all about the rise and fall of world empires. In verses 34 and 35 it describes a rock, 'not cut out with human hands,' striking the feet of the statue, smashing them and causing the statue to fall and break in pieces. The rock then grew to fill the earth. This speaks of Jesus and the Kingdom of God.

God is a Rock of Victory that no-one, no king, no power, no kingdom can resist or stand against. God has secured victory over Satan, over death and over sin, through Jesus. No matter how things are going on earth, there will come a day when Jesus will return and overthrow all in authority and establish His reign of righteousness, justice and peace. It is only through Jesus that we can have a hope for the future. However, we can also know victory as we live out our lives now.

David defeated Goliath, not by using second hand earthly armour and weapons, but by using one of the five small stones or rocks he picked up from a stream. They were not made by human hands. God gave him victory because of his faith. We can also know victory because Jesus has been victorious. Our five small stones for use against the enemy are, the Word of God, our Testimony, the Blood of Jesus, the Name of Jesus and the Praise of Jesus - all topics for another day. Suffice to know we have weapons in God which are mighty to defeat the enemy (see 2 Corinthians 10 v 4/5).

Reflection on Christian Character

Introduction

My experience has been that God inspires sermons in many different ways. It could be from a piece of scripture or bible story, a piece of music or a song, an experience or situation that has been encountered, or from an idea or picture that pops into one's head. This reflection about an arrow came from the later. One day, out of the blue, a picture of an arrow just popped into my head. As I couldn't shake this of, I believed the picture was from God and so gave it a lot of thought. This showed me that arrows could be representative of Christians and of their character and function. My rationale is that in Psalm 127 v 3 – 5, children are likened to arrows and in the gospel of St John 1 v 12 – 13 Christians are referred to as children of God. Putting these together Christians can be likened to arrows in God's hand.

Christian Character

An arrow has four component parts:
the shaft,
the arrowhead,
the fletching (or feathers)
and the nock.
Each of these can relate to
an element of
Christian character.

The Arrow Shaft

An arrow shaft has to be straight, smooth and strong, giving it the ability to fly true. In biblical times it was made of wood, which had to be chosen from the right type of tree, cut and then pared using a knife to cut away any bumps and imperfections. In the same way Christians need to be 'straight'. By this I mean honest, truthful and reliable in terms of what they say and do. It is in this context that Jesus, as the True Vine, talks about believers being pruned so that they can bring forth more and much fruit.

This can be a painful process. Jesus said, "let your yes be yes and your no be no," and, "let your light (or righteousness) shine before men." With this in mind, we need to be truthful and not deceitful in what we say to others. People need to know that we are dependable and can be relied upon and they can have confidence in us. Let us not be like the Pharisees that Jesus openly criticised for being hypocrites. People who said the right things but inwardly were empty of compassion, mercy and love for those in need. Christians are hand chosen by God and pruned by Him so that character grows and fruitfulness increases. In Proverbs it says that God chastens and corrects those that he loves, because he wants them to be straight and true. God wants genuine people who live out a life pleasing to him that impacts others.

The Arrowhead

The head or blade of an arrow has to be sharp and strong in order to be effective and to penetrate. In biblical times it was made of metal, which was strengthened by refining it in the fire to remove any impurities. Malachi likens Jesus to a refiner's fire which purifies and strengthens. As Christians we need to be purified and made strong. We are purified through the sacrifice and blood of Jesus, because of God's mercy and grace. This is not a one off experience, but has to be part of our Christian living. Invariably at times we will get it wrong, we will sin, but our purity can be re-established and maintained by confessing our sins and receiving God's forgiveness because His mercies are new every morning.

We are strengthened because of the help God provides when we face trouble and hard times in life. Paul talks about rejoicing in tribulations, sufferings or testing times, because tribulation leads to patience and perseverance, which leads to character and experience, which leads to hope, which doesn't disappoint (Romans 5 v 3 -5). God produces inner strength and faith in us when he helps us to overcome hardship. Therefore, to be effective, we have to be pure and to have experienced the strength and faith that comes from relying on God and His word.

To be sharp and able to penetrate situations we also need to know and to speak God's word at the appropriate time, not just from a head knowledge of the word, but a heart knowledge from experience that will generate faith and hope in others and cause change. In the book of Hebrews (chapter 4 v 12) it says that the word of God is living and active, sharper than any double-edged sword and therefore able to penetrate and prick consciences. That is the type of sharpness we need in our Christian lives. Our words are important. In Proverbs (18 v 21) it says there is death and life in the power of the tongue. Let's therefore speak to build up people's faith, not tear it down.

The Arrow Fletching

Fletchings, or feathers, are vitally important on an arrow, for their purpose is to ensure that the arrow doesn't deviate in flight, stays on the right path and therefore finds the desired target. As Christians we need to stay focused and on the right path, so that we find ourselves in those places where God wants us to be, both spiritually and naturally. This is God's desire for us and so the Holy Spirit has been released to lead us, guide us, teach us and comfort us on our pathway. Paul says in Romans 8 v 14 that, "For as many as are led by the Spirit of God, they are the sons of God." So how can we be led by the Holy Spirit?

As an arrow has a number of feathers on it, so too Christians have been provided with a number of ways to hear God and know the Spirit's prompting:

• We can pray, even when we don't know what to say. Paul in Romans 8 v 26 says that the Spirit helps us in prayer and intercedes for us with groans that words can't express.

• We can read and meditate on God's word and find truth, direction and encouragement in it, for after all it is a living word.

• We can attend church and listen intently to the sermons being preached.

• We can listen to Christian music and worship God and find inspiration.

• We can fellowship with other Christians and be moved by their testimony.

In all these God can help us move in the right direction and find our place in Him. He will confirm His will to us by sealing it with His peace, an inner peace. In terms of character, staying on right path means faithfulness and commitment.

The Arrow Nock

The nock can easily be overlooked or forgotten about. It is the small grove cut into the base of the shaft that the bow string fits into. It gives the arrow a degree of stability when it is being fired, as it stops the arrow slipping or moving when the bow string is being pulled back just before the arrow is released. It is about staying in the right place, the place where the archer wants it to be. In terms of Christian character I feel this speaks about Christians remaining faithful and being obedient, humble and submissive in God's hands. It is not about weakness but rather strength in control. Jesus was a strong person with a strong will and strong character, yet He remained totally submissive to His Father's will all through His life on earth. Because He did this the bible says that God highly exalted Him and gave Him a name above every name.

Paul tells us that we are to have the mind that Jesus had when he humbled himself

to serve, to wash feet and even die on the cross. Are we prepared to humble ourselves, die to self and set aside our preferences in order to serve others, forgive others and befriend others? Jesus said, "For whosoever shall save his life shall lose it and whosoever will lose his life for my sake shall find it." If you want to preserve your way of living and focus only on yourself, then you will lose the life that God wants you to have. You will miss out on the joy, the peace, the comfort, the sense of achievement and the strength He gives. Through obedience and faithfulness know security, the love of God and His purpose for your life.

Reflection on 'Function'

One thing to bear in mind concerning arrows is that the archer is the one who decides distance, direction and function. In the same way God decides when, where and how He wants His people to be used. For some it is within their family, their local church or their local community. For others it is the other side of the world. However, the distance and direction travelled is not the important element, it is whether the arrow has fulfilled its purpose and been successful. Don't long for foreign mission fields when God has chosen to use you at home. It is better to be successful and effective in the role and place you have been appointed, rather than unfulfilled and fruitless in a far-off land.

In terms of this reflection an arrow has three main uses: a weapon of attack, a means of defence and as a sign which gives direction.

An Arrow as a Weapon of Attack

When we read about the life of Jesus it is clear that He was on the attack or the offensive on numerous occasions. He attacked those who attempted to defraud and enslave others by their words and actions, such as the money changers and the hypocritical Pharisees. He attacked the self-righteous, those who were keen to accuse and punish others, but  ignoring their own sin. He attacked physical and mental illness on behalf of others, bringing healing. Jesus attacked death itself, raising people back to life.

This idea of attacking what was wrong was conveyed to His disciples and followers so that they in turn would carry on His Kingdom message in word and deed. Through the name of Jesus His followers were able to attack ignorance and indifference to the Gospel by speaking out the Gospel message with boldness and thus seeing many receive salvation. They were able to speak truth and justice in difficult situations as the Holy Spirit gave them the words to say. Through Jesus' name His followers were able to heal the sick and set the oppressed free.

The Gospel wasn't and shouldn't be passive. It should attack wrong and hurt and bring about change. I believe we have to be prepared to do the same. To speak up for others and attack injustice, discrimination and inequality on their behalf. It is good to know that God has used Christians to attack injustice and bring about change in society all throughout history. Christians have attacked and defeated such things as slavery, racial discrimination, exploitation of children and social injustice. God wants to use His people as a weapon to attack wrongdoing in society and bring about peace.

An Arrow as a Defence

Scripture tells us that one day a woman caught in the act of adultery was brought before Jesus by her accusers. No doubt they were attempting to make Jesus look bad by getting Him to either condemn the woman by agreeing with the law that she should die, or by disregarding the law and setting her free. Jesus knew that the law demanded her death but by His words and actions Jesus defended the woman and disarmed her accusers.

Have you ever thought about what He wrote on the ground in front of them all when he stooped down? Maybe He listed the sins of the woman's accusers: theft, dishonouring parents, using God's name wrongly and speaking untruths. Whatever Jesus wrote and did, He was able to stand up and speak out an inspired response that disarmed the accusers.

Many times in the Gospels we see Jesus forgiving and restoring people. It tells us in John 3 v 17 that. "God didn't send Jesus into the world to condemn the world but to save the world through Him." Jesus now stands before God as our mediator to defend us against the ultimate accuser, Satan. Like Jesus therefore, we are meant to defend the helpless and offer protection to the weak. James tells us that, "Pure religion is to visit (defend) the fatherless and widows in their affliction." Let's not side with accusers, those who criticise and are quick to condemn others, but rather speak up for the defenceless and the oppressed and pray for those who have lost their way.

An Arrow as a Sign

As well as being a means of attack and defence, an arrow can act as a sign that gives direction. If we are willing to go, God can 'fire' us into places or give us opportunities to provide direction and guidance to others. What could this mean for us?

Firstly, I believe it means we should be willing and able to point out the way to salvation to others and share our testimony to those willing to listen, concerning the goodness and reality of God. Saint Peter says (1 Peter 3 v 15), "Be ready always to give an answer to every man that asks you about the hope that you have." We must know that salvation is through faith in Jesus and not of works. If asked, would you be able to lead someone to Jesus?

Secondly, we need to be honest and to speak the truth in love, the aim being to win people over, not drive them away. In John 3 v 16 it clearly talks about God's love and sacrifice for the whole of mankind. However, it says that God wanted no one to perish. Therefore, the possibility of perishing is a reality and there is grave danger for those who do not believe on Jesus and accept Him. This needs to be told, just as much as 'the nice bit', but with compassion. I remember driving down the Shankill Road and having to stop at traffic lights. A man wearing a religious bib approached the car and started to shout through a megaphone that I was going to hell if I didn't accept Christ. There was no compassion, only judgement in his voice and the experience just turned me off.

Thirdly, as well as being able to point out the way to salvation and the consequence of rejecting it, we are also meant to demonstrate the right way to live in word and deed. Jesus said His followers were lights in the world and according to Peter meant to display the character of God through our lives (1

Peter 2 v 9). As such we need to live right, not just by avoiding wrongdoing, but by showing love, goodness, acceptance, generosity, compassion and forgiveness to friends and neighbours.

Lastly, I believe we are meant to point out the danger of falling away or turning away from God, because there are grave consequences. Hebrews 6 v 4 – 6 says, "It is impossible for those who have been enlightened, tasted of the heavenly gift, experienced the Holy Spirit and tasted of the goodness of God's word to be brought back to repentance if they fall away, because they are crucifying the Son of God again." Let's provide help and support to those struggling in their faith, even if it is through distant prayer because they don't want direct help.

Are you hitting the target?

Reflection on The Widow of Nain

Introduction

The story concerning the Widow of Nain and the intervention of Jesus to raise her son from the dead (as found in Luke 7 v 11 – 17), reveals the heart of God for those in distress and feeling hopeless. As such it has a message of hope for us all.

Jesus Sees the Individual

In the early part of Luke chapter 7 we are told that Jesus was heading to Nain from Capernaum, where he had healed the servant of a Roman Centurion. As Capernaum was about 25 miles north of Nain, the journey would have taken some time, given it would have been on foot. Luke tells us that Jesus wasn't alone, His disciples were travelling with Him, plus a large crowd, no doubt eager and excited to see what else Jesus would do. As Jesus approached the gate of the town of Nain, he came across the funeral procession of a widow's only son and that a large crowd was with her. The bible says that when Jesus saw her, His heart went out to her and he said, "Don't Cry." In spite of the large crowd travelling with Jesus, and the one in front of Him that made up the funeral procession, he was able to see and focus on one woman who was desperately in need of comfort and help.

Jesus isn't concerned with crowds, rather, He is concerned about the individuals that make up the crowd, especially those in need of help. Jesus sees us all as individuals not just someone who is part of a crowd, a church or even a family. God sees you, even when you want to hide from Him. Jonah  found this to be true when he tried to run away from God. God saw him and watched over him, even when he ended up inside the great fish. David in Psalm 139 makes it perfectly clear that God sees us no matter where we are or where we go. There is no escape from the gaze of God. Isn't this good to know? For when we find ourselves in difficulty and feeling lost, God sees us and will come to speak comfort and to restore.

Jesus Knows the Individual

I believe that when Jesus saw the woman, even without being told, He knew what her situation was and why help was so desperately needed. He seen beyond what his eyes could see. He seen beyond the physical and natural. Without being told, Jesus knew that she was a widow and that the dead person was her only son. He seen that she would be left alone with no-one to support her in her old age. He seen that the son's death meant the future loss of her family name as there was no-one to carry it on and the loss of the family's land and inheritance. Her future was bleak and seemingly hopeless. Is it any wonder that Jesus' heart went out to her?

We need to know that Jesus, in spite of whatever is going on around us, not only sees us in times of need and distress but knows what we are going through and the pain we suffer. He doesn't just see the immediate situation and plan a quick fix, rather He sees the future and does what is really best for us in the long term. Sometimes we don't understand or appreciate this, so we complain when things don't work out as we want and when we want.

Jesus knows all about us, even those secret fears and worries that we keep hidden within ourselves. The bible tells us that Jesus calls His sheep by name and that our names are written on God's hands (Luke 10 v 20). Jesus knows where you are and your deepest needs. As such His heart goes out to you and all who are suffering because He is full of compassion and love.

Jesus Aids the Individual

The story goes on that Jesus touched the coffin and those carrying it stood still. Jesus isn't content just to see you or to know you, He wants to touch you and bring about change and give new life. The bible doesn't tell us why the pallbearers stopped, but I am assuming that word had gotten out as to who Jesus was from his disciples and the crowd that was following Him. There must have been an air of expectation because of the reputation and authority of Jesus. Jesus didn't disappoint. He knew who He was and who His Father was. He knew He was the Son of God, The Resurrection and the Life and that He had authority and power to deal with the need in front of him.

Nothing is too big for God. Jesus is still the Resurrection and The Life and can speak life into dead situations. The thing that speaks to me about this story is that Jesus didn't stop the coffin because it was an opportunity to give more proof of who He was and to receive more praise. He didn't stop because it was a chance to win more converts and to silence doubters. Rather, the bible says that when Jesus saw the woman His heart went out to her. The thing that caused Jesus to stop the coffin was love and compassion. He saw the woman's tears. He wasn't thinking about the disciples or the crowd, or trying to please them. He wasn't thinking about His reputation. His only focus was upon helping a poor widow who had lost everything and who was in deep distress and grief.

That's the message of the Gospel, "For God so loved the world that He gave His son." God's actions towards us are based on love. The bible clearly says that 'God is Love' (1 John 2 v 8) and according to King David (Ps 36 v 7) "God's unfailing love is priceless". We have to understand that everything God has done and will do for us is out of love and that He will forever continue to aid and help us.

When Jesus touched the coffin and the pallbearers stopped, Jesus spoke directly to the dead man. He said, "Young man, I say to you, get up." Luke tells us that the man then sat up and began to talk and that the crowd were in awe because Jesus had brought the dead to life. We need to know that today Jesus is still very much in the business of breathing life into dead situations. He is still The Resurrection and The Life. If your spiritual life is dead or is dying, if your hope and faith in God has diminished, if your excitement and enthusiasm has waned, God wants to stop you and speak new life into your heart and soul.

Jesus Restored the Individual

Finally, Luke tells us that after the young man was raised to life, Jesus gave him back to his mother. To me this is significant. Even though the young man may have wanted to, Jesus didn't ask him to join His group of disciples and to follow after Him. What He wanted and did, was to give the son back to his widowed mother so that they could have a new, fresh start and the family unit restored. Jesus wanted the woman to have hope for the future, to know that the family name would live on and that the family's ancestral land wouldn't be lost. He wanted her peace restored. He also wanted a son restored to his mother and a mother reunited with her son. It was God who instigated family and family life and so Jesus wanted to preserve it.

Today Jesus still cares about family and family relationships. He wants sons and daughters reunited with parents. He wants brothers reunited with sisters. He wants parents honoured by their children and children nurtured and developed by their parents out of love. Jesus wants to mend broken and dead relationships and give renewed hope to families. To those who wish they could have a fresh start in a relationship, the good news is they can if they are prepared to stop, listen the voice of Jesus and respond to it.

The other aspect in this story is that becoming a Christian isn't necessarily about going off to foreign lands as a missionary or preacher. It can be about being a supportive loving member of a family and living out your Christian faith at home and in your community. God gives to families, he doesn't take away.

Reflection on Water into Wine

Introduction

Turning water into wine was the first public miracle that Jesus performed. It is found in John 2 v 1 – 11. Given all the things that He could have done to start His ministry and raise His profile, this miracle seems rather unusual. However, I believe it is significant and sets the scene for what was to come. It contrasts with the first public miracle of Moses, where water was turned into blood, signifying the Old Covenant of required blood sacrifice and strict obedience to law, rules and custom. When Jesus turned water to wine it was symbolic of the New Covenant where only faith was needed to experience the forgiveness of God and the freedom and celebration that goes with it, as represented by the wine.

Seek God's Will

The first thing to note is that Jesus wouldn't be pressurised by family or friends into doing something which He felt may not be sanctioned by God, or in line with God's timing. When Jesus was approached by his mother to tell him that the wine had ran out (or was running out) he mildly rebuked her. Why? Jesus needed to check what His heavenly Father's will was. He needed approval to begin His earthly ministry. He needed to know if the request, or its timing, was in line with God's wishes. Jesus wasn't prepared to rush into something just to please people, even His mother. His only objective was to do the will of his heavenly Father. Jesus did eventually act and turn water into wine to meet a specific need, but on His terms and when he felt the timing was right.

As a Christian, we can be pressurised by people to do things or to act in a certain way. It maybe to take up a position within the church or local community. Perhaps it is to give of our time, money and/or ability to a good cause. However, we need to be careful, just as Jesus was, to do the God thing. Accepting a role and responsibility for the wrong reason or agreeing to do something because it seems good, can lead to dis-peace and cause anxiety and stress. God wants us to know peace in our lives and so He points to Jesus as our example. Jesus paused until he knew what the right course of action was, and so He wants us to be discerning in terms of our actions.

In my Christian life I have had to learn to say no, or not at the minute, as well as saying yes. As a young Christian I practically said yes to everything and took too much on board, which many times robbed me of peace by putting me under pressure and stress, leading to friction within my family life. God wants us to know that it's not unchristian to say, "no or not at the moment". Jesus did it many times when people asked him for a sign. So let's exercise caution before jumping into things. Let's wait on God, not run ahead of Him.

Seek the Approval of God not Man.

When Jesus performed the miracle, He wasn't seeking fame, human praise and public recognition. The miracle wasn't performed in Jerusalem, the capital city, the City of God. It wasn't performed in the Temple, a place of pilgrimage. Rather, it took place in a small remote insignificant village called Cana, about five miles from Nazareth, where Jesus had been raised. Even there it wasn't in the synagogue or the market place where people could see it, but at a family wedding. Jesus didn't change the water to wine in front of the guests, or walk in with the wine declaring what he had done. No, He simply told the servants what to do and then to take the 'wine' to the steward and say nothing.

Many times in scripture we read of Jesus telling people who he had healed not to say anything or point Him out. In the Sermon on the Mount, Jesus gave instructions to the crowds to be careful not to do their good works and acts of righteousness before men and not to announce them as the Pharisees did to be honoured of men. Rather, Jesus said when you help the needy (not if you help the needy) don't let your right hand know what your left hand is doing (Matt 6 v 1 - 4). God sees what we do in secret and will reward us. This defined Jesus' ministry. He was concerned with others and not himself. Because he humbled himself, even to death on a cross, God highly exalted him and gave him a name above all names. The same can be true for us. God wants us to do good works, to help those in need, but not for recognition or the praise of men but rather because that is what God has put in our hearts.

Seek God's Generosity and Thoughtfulness

This miracle was very practical in nature but also symbolic. At the wedding there was a real practical need as the wine had, or was just about to, run out. This practical side of Jesus' ministry is real and relevant. It was seen in feeding the 5000 and getting the fishermen to cast their nets into the sea after a fruitless night of fishing and ending up with a massive catch that their nets couldn't hold. Yes, Jesus is primarily concerned with spiritual matters. He did come to seek and save sinners from sin. He wants to give forgiveness, to apply grace and give peace. But he was and still is concerned with our practical needs. God has always demonstrated this. In the OT God helped Daniel and his friends with their education, so that they became the best students. He gave Joseph the administrative and practical ability to help run a household then a country. God, through Elisha, allowed a widow to fill all the pots she could get her hands on with oil, so she could provide for her family. In my career, against all the odds, I ended up as part of a senior manager team in a successful international company. Many times I had to seek God for help as to how to do things, how to write an important report, how to bring about successful business changes that increased efficiency and profitability and how to manage people to bring out their best. God

is concerned with your everyday life and is willing to help in terms of employment, career, education, financial planning, relationships, etc., not just to get by, but to succeed.

Jesus didn't turn the water into any old wine, but the best. Jesus didn't make just enough wine but an abundance of wine, about 900 bottles. Enough so that there would be wine left over that could be shared with others, given away and even sold. The life Jesus gives us is an abundant life that fully satisfies us and that can overflow to touch others.

In terms of the wedding, running out of wine would have caused great embarrassment and shame to the wedding party as wine was a key element at a wedding, symbolising joy, blessing and the union between the bride and bridegroom. A shortage would also have posed a question over whether the bridegroom could support his wife and a family financially. Because Jesus didn't want the family shamed or doubts raised about the future success of the marriage He intervened. God doesn't want us shamed or embarrassed as we travel through life, so He intervenes.

Seek God's Infilling and Transformation

In the miracle, Jesus used empty earthenware jars that were traditionally used in Jewish custom for ceremonial washing in terms of purification. They would never have had wine in them. At Jesus instruction, these jars were filled only with fresh water which Jesus then transformed into wine. This is remarkable because water doesn't contain all the elements necessary for making wine, let alone good wine. It only contains the elements of hydrogen and oxygen. There are no colouring, or flavouring components in water to make it look, smell and taste good. There are no carbon molecules required to make alcohol. All these had to be created by Jesus out of nothing, in the same way that God created the earth out of nothing. It shows the supernatural power of God that Jesus demonstrated time and time again during His ministry. Jesus didn't multiply old dregs of wine but created totally new wine that was seen as the best.

Paul likens Christians to earthen jars containing a treasure. When we come to Jesus, he fills us afresh, cleanses us from all our sin and then transforms us, making each of us into a new creation. It is a miracle of God's grace and mercy. It is God who brings about the change and transformation, causing us to act, speak and think differently. If you are feeling drained and empty, Jesus will can, and will, fill you afresh. Firstly, with water to cleanse, purify and remove sin, but then He will bring about transformation, creating new wine of the Spirit to bring renewed joy and gladness into your life that can overflow and impact others. God says, "Behold I make all things new." God doesn't just make some things new but all things. Whatever needs renewing in your life and circumstances, God can do it.

Reflection on God being a Consuming Fire

Introduction

God is described in many ways all through the bible. For example, his people have referred to Him as a strong tower, a deliverer, a shepherd, a redeemer and a father.

All these give comfort because they describe God in a way that show He helps, defends and protects us. However, there is one descriptor of God, found in both the Old and New Testament (Deuteronomy 4 v 9 - 24 & 9 v 1 - 6 and Hebrews 12 v 29), which used to scare and puzzle me. It is God being described as 'A Consuming Fire', which at first sight depicts a God focused on judgement, punishment and destruction. However, there is much more to see concerning the Fire of God.

The Reality of Judgement and Escape

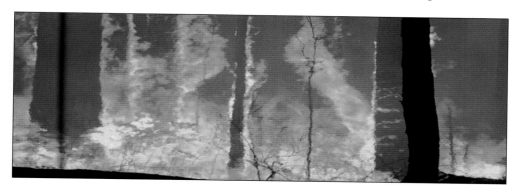

One can easily see the reality of God's punishment through fire in the story of Sodom and Gomorrah. Here God destroyed those cities and their inhabitants with fire because of their wickedness and sin. In the New Testament Jesus told many parables that referred to God's judgement and punishment. Parables such as the sheep and the goats, the wheat and the tares and the unforgiving servant. This theme of punishment for the unrighteous, the unbelieving and the unrepentant runs all through the New Testament, being mentioned in the Four Gospels, Thessalonians, Hebrews, Jude and Revelation and is an unescapable truth, as is Hell. It is something we must accept and believe, but in doing so it makes the sacrifice of Jesus even more remarkable in that we can escape the judgement and wrath of a righteous and holy God by simply believing in and accepting Jesus as our Saviour. The reality is, that although God is a consuming fire, He wants no-one to perish. This is the message in John 3 v 16. We can escape the fire of God, the wrath and punishment of God simply by putting our faith in Jesus.

The burning bush that Moses saw gives us a picture of this. God didn't destroy or consume the bramble bush even though it was full of thorns and growing wild. No, God knew fruit was possible and so He saved it from the fire. God also knows fruit is possible in us, in mankind, and so He restrains His consuming fire, waiting on our repentance and acceptance of Jesus.

However, there is more to fire than just destruction. For example, it can give light in darkness, bring warmth and comfort, forge and refine objects and act as a weapon and means of defense. These are all attributes we can find in God as seen below.

God's Fire as a Guide and Weapon

When the Children of Israel left Egypt, God led them with a cloud and a pillar of fire. This not only directed their path, but also formed a hedge of defense behind them when they rested, thus protecting them from the enemies that were following them. Then, as God's people began to possess the Promised Land, God said to them (in Deuteronomy 9) that He would go before them as a consuming

fire to destroy their enemies, to defeat them and drive them out. Today God still wants to lead His people in the right direction so that they can find green pastures and still waters that nourish and refresh. He wants to lead His children to new opportunities where they can find fruit and produce fruit and be successful. He wants to defend and comfort His people so that their souls can be restored and that peace of mind can be regained. He wants to defeat their enemies and drive them away so that victory can be experienced.

If you are struggling today with what path to follow, God's word can be a lamp to your feet and a light to your path (Psalm 119 v 5). Jesus is still 'The Way' and the Good Shepherd who leads in the right direction. If you are struggling with habits, even addictions that seem to control you and take away your peace, then let God lead you and fight on your behalf to regain freedom. God can be a fire that leads and frees.

God's Fire as a means of Refining

Scripture refers to God as a refiner's fire (Malachi 3 v 2&3). In refining precious metals like gold and silver, fire is used to remove impurities and to increase their value. With metals like iron and steel, fire is used to toughen and strengthen. Many prophets refer to this process declaring that God refines His people. Here fire is not used to destroy but rather to remove sin and wrongdoing so as to increase holiness and worth.

We start of as precious to God in Jesus but He wants to increase our worth and value. Like the hardening of steel God wants to strengthen us so we can battle and retain our faith, even when things get tough. God never promised an easy life in Christ. However, He did say He would be with us in times of trouble. God uses hard times to refine and strengthen us. Paul says in Romans 5 v 3 & 4, "Rejoice in our sufferings, because we know that suffering produces perseverance; perseverance character and character hope. And hope does not disappoint us or make us ashamed." Likewise in Proverbs 3 v 11 & 12 it says, "My son, despise not the chastening of the Lord, neither be weary of His correction: For whom the Lord loves he corrects, even as a father the son in whom He delights." If you are going through hard times know that God is

with you to bring you through them and that He may be using them to refine you so that you become even more precious and stronger.

God's Fire as a means of Encouraging

After the resurrection of Jesus, He walked and talked with some disciples as they travelled to Emmaus. The disciples were confused, fearful and sad. They didn't know what to believe or what the future held for them. On the journey they didn't recognize Jesus but felt something deep inside themselves as they travelled and talked together. It was only after Jesus broke bread with them that they recognized who He was and later spoke to each other about their hearts being greatly moved and burning within them as Jesus spoke to them and opened up the scriptures (Luke 24 v 32). The fire of God had rekindled something, caused hope to rise and brought a sense of excitement to the disciples. God's fire can do the same with us. If we read His word, walk with Him and listen, our hearts can be moved and made to burn within us. We can feel the same as Charles Wesley when he said that, "he felt his heart strangely warmed." If you have grown cold, if your heart is lukewarm, rather than being fearful and downcast, be glad that the fire of God can ignite your passion and give you a renewed sense of love for Him. The closer you get the warmer you will feel.

God's Fire as a means of Motivating

The book of Acts tells us about the time that the disciples were in an upper room waiting together, as Jesus had instructed them, for the promise of the Holy Spirit. Scripture tells us that as they waited tongues like fire descended and rested on each of them. Note that none were overlooked or missed out. The fire of God had descended. As a result, any fear of declaring what they believed in disappeared. The disciples were inspired, stimulated and fully motivated, causing them to leave the upper room and rush into the market place to praise

God. Even the criticism and scorn of some people didn't put them of and led Peter to preach out the gospel message with power and authority. Thousands believed and turned to Jesus.

This is the impact the fire of God can have. If you are fearful or embarrassed about sharing your faith or proclaiming the gospel, ask for the fire of God to descend and rest on you. Be prepared for an inner transformation and an explosion of your faith. Our God is a Consuming Fire, that's why John the Baptist said Jesus would baptise with fire and the Holy Spirit. Let Him burn away all that is wrong in us and ignite all that is good, so we can live out the gospel without fear or embarrassment.

Reflection on Jesus Saves

If you are like me, then when you have been out and about, either walking or driving, you will have noticed signs on trees, telegraph poles, lamp posts, etc. containing the message, 'Jesus Saves.' Normally, probably like many people, I would just glance at these and not give the message much thought. However, one day when seeing this message, I felt prompted to pause and think about this statement. I was surprised at what I believe God showed me in terms of, 'What Jesus saves us from and for?'

Saved from the Eternal Consequence of Sin

In terms of what Jesus saves us from, the obvious answer, which is fundamental and traditional within Christianity, is that Jesus saves those who believe in Him from sin. He is only one who can save people from sin and its primary consequences. He alone, because of His sacrificial death on the cross, can cleanse us and thus save us from God's judgement and punishment, spiritual death and total eternal exclusion from the presence of a Holy God. He is the only cure for sin and the only way to God. That's why He said He was The Way, The Truth and The Life.

Any other message or Gospel is untrue and contrary to God's word and plan. No amount of good works, charitable giving, church attendance or penance will save people from their sin. As John the Baptist said, "Jesus is The Lamb of God who takes away the sin of the world." (John 1 v 29 & 36)

I knew this truth from an early age but kept putting of making a commitment to Jesus until I was 25 years old. Looking back now, it was such a waste. I was afraid of how my friends would react and what they would say. In many ways I was more afraid of them than of God. However, God didn't give up on me. When I finally accepted Jesus on Easter Sunday 1975, I felt a real sense of peace, relief and happiness. My fear of others disappeared. If you haven't accepted Jesus yet, He wants to save you from sin and an eternity of regret.

Saved from the Temporal Consequences of Sin

Although the primary and central message of the Gospel is salvation and freedom from sin, there is much more contained within the message 'Jesus Saves' than at first sight. Adam's initial disobedience to God brought sin into the world and since then an explosion of sinful actions which now affect the whole of mankind. To put it into God speak, "All have sinned and fallen short of the glory of God." (Romans 3 v 23) The escalation of sinful actions can be seen in the first few chapters of Genesis where disobedience led to accusation, blame shifting, lying, jealousy, cheating and murder. With these actions came many consequences which plague us today, such as embarrassment, shame, guilt, fear, sorrow, pain and physical death.

The good news is that Jesus came to help save us from these as well as from spiritual death. This is seen all throughout His ministry where he: brought healing from physical and mental illness; accepted those who came to Him thus dealing with their isolation; spoke comfort, encouragement and forgiveness; and turned people's lives around for the better.

The prophet Isaiah is clear about this. In Isaiah chapter 53 the prophet declares that Jesus would take up our infirmities, carry our sorrows and bring healing through His wounds. In chapter 61 he further says that Jesus would bind up the broken hearted, liberate captives from whatever robs them of freedom (habits, addictions or fears), bring comfort, restore joy and happiness, open blind eyes, and so much more. Jesus came to SAVE US from the physical and emotional consequences of sin. His ministry on earth was about healing, forgiving and restoring. This ministry hasn't changed and we can benefit from it today.

I am not saying everything will be made perfect and all our problems will disappear, but at least we will have hope and someone to stand with us when comfort and strength are needed.

Saved from Defeat by the Enemy

Whether a football fan or not, I am sure you will have heard of Pat Jennings, who had a long and distinguished career as a goalkeeper. His job was to prevent the opposition (the enemy) scoring goals against his team and thus avoiding defeat. In short, he had to make saves.

In life we have one primary enemy, Satan, who is always trying to score against us. His aim is to steal, kill and destroy our faith, our hope, our motivation, our dreams, as well as our lives. This enemy wants to score goals against us, to defeat us and rob of our faith and our hope in God. He will use any means to achieve this, bringing temptation to test our resolve and invading our minds to create uncertainty and fear, causing us to even doubt our faith and the existence of God. I know, I've been there.

However, scripture tells us (1 Corinthians 10 v 13) that Jesus limits the temptations we face. Jesus ensures that we will not be overwhelmed or face what God knows we cannot bear. Jesus saves us and prevents the enemy scoring goals

that will defeat us. Being tempted isn't sin, after all Jesus was tempted. It is giving in to temptation that is the problem. When we pray the Lord's Prayer we are acknowledging this, for we pray, "save us from temptation and deliver us from evil."

But there is more. God has given us armour to help us stand firm and ensure that the enemy doesn't score against us. This armour (see Ephesians 6 v 10 – 18), when we put it on, protects our whole being. The belt of truth holds all together and allows us to be secure in God. The breastplate protects our heart and emotions, saving us from feelings of guilt, shame and fear. The helmet protects our minds, allowing us to think clearly and to know the reality of God, the One who gives soundness of mind. The shoes help us walk along the right path, avoiding pitfalls and places we shouldn't be. The shield stops the lies, accusations and finger pointing of Satan, thus protecting our faith and identity in God. The sword, which is the Word of God, reveals truth and cuts through all the enemy's lies and half-truths. Unlike the best goalkeepers in the world, no-one has ever scored against Jesus. He remains triumphant and always alert to defend us.

Saved for Presentation

A few years ago an uncle of my wife, when in his eighties, became a Christian and then got married. Who says we can't have a fruitful life in old age? Sadly, he has now passed away. One of the things he was passionate about was collecting or saving stamps. Many times, when we visited, he took out his collection and took pride in showing it off to us. Every stamp was important to him and had its unique place in one of his many albums. He knew all about them, where they came from, their value and many unusual facts about them.

In John chapter 15 it tells us that Jesus has chosen, or saved, us to be His and to bear fruit. Because we belong to Him, He takes pride in us and wants to show us of. As a young boy, whenever teams were being picked, I was usually the last one chosen. It was embarrassing. Therefore, it's great to know that Jesus has picked or chosen me to be part of His team, not because I am the only one left but because He really wants me. Although part of a larger collection (The Church) He knows us all as individuals, knowing our names and even the very number of hairs on our heads. Scripture says that Jesus wants to present us to His Father, not to show up our faults but because he loves us and is proud of us. We are the reason He came to earth. In the book of Jude it talks about us being presented to God as faultless. In Ephesians it talks about us being presented as a glorious church, not having any spot or wrinkle or blemish. Jesus takes pride in us, he sees us as special and precious, sees things in us that we can't see or even imagine, that's why He presents us to God.

Jesus also wants to present or show us to the world. That's why Jesus calls us salt and the light of the world. That's why Paul says, "We are called out of darkness into light to show forth the virtues and nature of God." Paul tells Christians to present their bodies as a living sacrifice. Jesus wants the world to see God in us and to see what God can do in us and through us. If you have low self-esteem, maybe a lack of confidence, take comfort in knowing that Jesus sees worth in you, has chosen you and wants to show you of to God and to the world.

Saved for an Eternal Future

On a hot summer's day (to be honest on most days) I love to buy a large 99 cone, full of whipped ice cream with a chocolate flake in it. Because I like to save the

best till last, I push the flake down as far as it will go into the cone, eat the top layer of ice cream, and then enjoy eating the flake, crunchy cone and ice cream all together.

At times Jesus saved the best till last. The wedding feast at Cana, where He turned water into wine is an example. The wine He created was the best wine and in abundance (about 900 bottles). Saint Paul in 1 Corinthians 2 v 9 tells us that, "No eye has seen, no ear has heard, no mind has conceived what God has prepared (or saved) for those who love Him." Jesus is saving the best till last for us.

Saint John tells us that Jesus is preparing a place for us, saving a place for us in heaven. It is not just any old place but a unique place, a place especially made and shaped for each of us because Jesus knows all about us, our preferences, our desires, our likes and dislikes. Jesus is saving up things for us that we can't even imagine. The Book of Revelation gives us a glimpse of what is to come when it talks about God's new heaven being a place where there are no more tears, death, mourning, crying or pain. That's a place I want to go to. I wonder what awaits us in eternity. I wonder what things Jesus is saving up for us. Suffice to know it will great and that Jesus is saving us for an eternity residing with Him.

Reflection on Psalm 23

Introduction

Psalm 23 is one of the best known pieces of scripture in the bible and probably could be recited word for word by many Christians and non-Christians alike. It has brought hope and comfort to many. However, because it is so well known there is a danger in thinking 'I've heard it all before' and to become complacent about the psalm and the truth it contains. This reflection looks at a few aspects of this psalm.

The Shepherd's Relationship

Let me start by saying that the word THE can be significant depending on where and how it is used. It can convey that someone or something is unique, special and unequalled. There are many examples of this, The Grand Canyon, The Great Wall of China, The Giant's Causeway, The Queen of England and The president of the USA. David starts this Psalm with the two words 'The Lord.' In doing so he was recognising and declaring that there is only one Lord and God, the one who created the heavens and earth, the one who is all powerful and above all gods. To him God was unique and unequalled, full of power and majesty. He was the great 'I Am' as depicted in Jesus.

However, in spite of this, David was able to say that this awesome Lord was his personal shepherd. He didn't say a shepherd but 'my' shepherd, a shepherd with whom he had a personal relationship. It's important to say that he wasn't boasting or showing off. He was simply testifying to a fact. All throughout his life God was with him to exalt him, lead him, protect him and to forgive and restore him.

For us, we can take comfort in knowing that this relationship isn't restrictive. That's why Jesus said He was the good shepherd who would give His life for the sheep - plural. Jesus is the good shepherd who calls His sheep by name and who seeks out those that are lost.

This Sovereign Lord, although exalted above every power and authority, wants a personal relationship with each one of us, irrespective of whether we are rich or poor, black or white, able bodied or disabled, intellectual or practical. All we have to do is accept His free gift of salvation and He will become our shepherd as He was David's. It is a choice, a decision that we all have to make. If we allow Jesus to become our shepherd the benefits are endless and eternal.

The Shepherd's Provision

At the start of the psalm David says that he will not be in want. I must admit I have struggled with this sentiment, for at times in his life David was definitely in want. At times he was hungry, he needed a place of safety to hide in, he was alone and wanted company. However, the thing that David never lacked was God's presence, God's protection, God's love and God's mercy and forgiveness. It is these things we will never lack when Jesus is our shepherd. Paul says that God's grace is always sufficient for us. The more grace we need the more is made available, it will never run out.

David goes on the say that the shepherd makes him to lie down. In life others may want to drive us and get their pound of flesh, but God makes us lie down and rest. He knows the value and importance of rest, for He rested after creating the heavens and the earth. He doesn't want us exhausting ourselves but wants us to be still at times and recharge our batteries. So, at times, God steps in to make us lie down and rest. Jesus said, "Come unto me and find rest for your souls."

The shepherd doesn't make us lie down anywhere but in green pastures and beside still waters, places of nourishment and refreshment. He leads to fresh, abundant green pasture where the sheep can be fed and satisfied and to still water where sheep can freely drink. It should be noted that the shepherd leads to green pastures and still waters, both plural. From time to time God intervenes and changes our circumstances so that we move on to a new pasture to receive fresh nourishment. This new pasture could be a new church, a new job, a new house, a new school or maybe a new relationship. Whatever the reason, God's desire is to restore your soul. He cares for your emotional needs and will help you deal with fears, worries and anxieties. Jesus as the shepherd wants to give peace of mind and to restore and repair the damage done by others who have been critical, judgemental and hurtful.

The Shepherd's Presence

Up to this point in the psalm David has been testifying to anyone who would listen about the shepherd and what He does. There is a lesson here for us all. How much testimony have we given about the shepherd? However, when David begins to talk about the 'valley of the shadow of death' he gets personal and begins to talk directly to the shepherd. He says, "You are with me…Your rod and staff they protect me… You prepare things for me (and) You anoint me." His testimony had led to a conversation (a prayer time) with God. If you struggle with prayer, think about all the things God has done for you and you will be naturally led to prayer.

David never said God would give a trouble free life, but he did say that God walked with him in times of trouble, especially in the valley. We all have valley experiences, but like David, God will walk with us through them. In Isaiah chapter 43, God makes a promise to His people and that now includes us. He says that when (not if) we pass through the waters he will be with us and that when we pass through rivers we will not be swept away. When we pass through fire we will not be burned or set ablaze. Yes, troubles may come, and we may get wet and hot, but we will survive it because God promises never to leave us or forsake us, no matter what the circumstances. Saint Paul declared that in our weakness God's strength is made perfect (2 Corinthians 12 v 9). God will uphold us, walk with us through troubled times and, even in death, will not desert us.

The Shepherd's Anointing

In the psalm, when talking to God, David says, "You anoint my head with oil, my cup runs over (or overflows)." The prophet Samuel at God's bidding anointed David with oil as a sign of future kingship and God's recognition. Jesus does the same for us. We are anointed as a mark of future kingship and God's acceptance of us. Saint Paul states this when writing to the church in Corinth (2 Corinthians 1 v 21/22). Jesus blesses us with gifts and abilities to use in His service. He gives abundantly. He makes us kings and priests. He doesn't hold back or drip feed us. The cup of anointing overflows.

However, there is more to the anointing than this. Shepherds, I am sure including David, used oil to anoint the head of sheep. Why? There are certain types of little flies that torment sheep by laying their eggs in their nostrils, which turn into worms and can burrow into the animal's brain. This can cause the sheep to bang their heads against posts or walls trying to get rid of the irritation. They can die from this. So the shepherd anoints their whole head with oil to act as a barrier, a shield, to give protection and bring ease and peace.

Have you ever felt like you were hitting your head against a wall? Are there things tormenting you and robbing you of peace? Let Jesus anoint your head with oil and give you ease.

When the shepherd rubs in the oil he also examines the sheep's head for cuts and wounds caused by hazards like thistles, rocks, sticks and predators. Even the greenest of pastures may have hazards. So shepherds check their sheep, looking for any wounds that need attention. They add oil to any wounds to bring healing, just like in the story of the Good Samaritan where he poured oil and wine on the robbed man's wounds.

We live in a dangerous world and can get wounded. One of the worst sayings from childhood is, "sticks and stones may break my bones, but words can never hurt me." Well, that's just not true. Words CAN and DO hurt us. They can cause wounds that can go much deeper than sticks and stones. Wounds that only the Good Shepherd can heal. The good shepherd can anoint our heads and bring healing from those things that have discouraged us and taken away self-confidence.

Reflection on Jesus healing a crippled woman

Introduction

In His three years of public ministry, Jesus demonstrated the power and majesty of a mighty God through the miracles and healings He performed, as well as his ability to teach deep truths about God in a practical and understandable way for ordinary people. As such, He gained recognition and fame throughout the land. However, to put it into Northern Ireland speak, 'He never let this go to His head,' and was always ready to help the poor and needy, as He still is today. This reflection focuses on how Jesus dealt with a woman who had been suffering for many years. It is found in Luke 13 v 10 – 17.

The priority of Jesus is on the Individual

Jesus, as he often did, was teaching in one of the synagogues on the Sabbath day. No doubt, given his reputation, there probably would have been a crowd listening to what He was saying and probably hoping to see Him do something extraordinary and miraculous. Because Jesus was teaching, He probably would have been concentrating on the subject matter, keen to get His message across concerning the Kingdom of God.

In the gathering was a woman who had been crippled for 18 years. Luke tells us that she was bent double and so it would have been a real strain and effort for her to look up and maybe she was unable to look into Jesus face. This poses a few questions for us. Do we get bent over at times because we are carrying burdens that prevent us looking up? Are we carrying so much worry, stress or sin that we can't look up to God? Are we weighed down and bent over with problems about relationships, finance and health? If so, know there is hope. The prophet Isaiah tells us a number of times that God makes the crooked straight.

In spite of the crowd and his focus on the teaching, Jesus saw the woman in the midst of the crowd. Yes, Jesus saw her disability, but He didn't see a cripple, He saw a person, an individual who had a need. To those around her, she may have

been insignificant, or maybe even an object of fun. But to Jesus, she was important and worth His time and effort. We may be part of a crowd, an organisation, a church, a family, but to Jesus, we are individuals needing His attention which He is so willing to give. Even if at times you can't look up, Jesus sees you and cares.

Jesus sees beyond the superficial

When Jesus sees someone, He sees beyond their outward appearance and sees what is on the inside. Saint John in Revelation describes Jesus as having, 'eyes like a blazing fire' (Revelation 1 v 14). As such they can cut through fog, mist and masks that we sometimes wear and see the truth.

Some time ago my granddaughter was looking for a new laptop computer for school. Her priorities were its colour (purple was her preference) and what dimensions it would have so that it would be easy to carry around. She totally missed the point that what was on the inside was the key to its usefulness. Features like its memory size, processing speed, installed software, operating system, etc. It took an expert to point this out and lead us to make the right decision about what to purchase. God looks beyond the physical and sees the heart and our potential. He is the expert on humanity. The good news is that God has chosen us, paying full price, not a discounted one.

When Jesus saw the woman He knew her state of her mind and the feelings of frustration, depression, hopelessness and desperation she had. He saw her life style, how she was treated and viewed by others and how she struggled to manage day by day chores. He saw her desire to be whole and her level of faith, maybe only the size of a mustard seed after eighteen years of suffering. In the same way Jesus sees and knows all about us and what we hope for.

When Jesus sees us He invites us to come

In the story, Luke tells us that after seeing the woman, Jesus called her to come to Him. This seems strange, given she was crippled, doubled in two and had to strain to look up. Surely it would have been much easier for Jesus to go to her. So why did He ask her to come to Him?

I don't believe it was to expose her and let all the crowd see her condition. I don't think it was to embarrass or humiliate her. I don't think it was to make things difficult for her or to parade her in front of everyone so that they could have a ringside seat for what was to come. Jesus never wants to shame or embarrass anyone of us. His aim is always to bless and restore.

I believe that when Jesus called her to come He wanted her to know that He had seen her, she was important to Him, even more important than Him continuing to teach and, lastly, to get her to release and exercise what faith she had. Many times Jesus called out for people to come. Jesus said, "Come unto me all ye that labour and are heavy laden and I will give you rest (Matt 11 v 28)." With Zacchaeus, Jesus said, "Come down, for I want to visit with you," and in doing so turned his life around. With Lazarus, Jesus called, "Come forth," and give him new life.

This same invitation 'to come' is given to us all. Like the crippled woman and all those others who have come willingly to Jesus, we have to make the decision to respond or not. To quote a tennis term, 'the ball is in our court.' If you want to be able to look up again, take the first step.

The result of coming to Jesus

When the woman responded to the invitation of Jesus and began to walk towards Him, Jesus said, "You are set free," and when close enough to Him Jesus laid his hands on her and she was immediately healed and able to straighten and stand tall as God intended. Her immediate response was to praise God, for she knew her healing was from God not man. In her joy the crowd became unimportant and in a sense disappeared. Things that previously would have held her back also disappeared and she was totally free to move. In Jesus getting the woman to come to Him, he got her to activate her faith.

For us to receive freedom and the ability 'to stand tall' in the face of difficult and trying circumstances, we need to heed the invitation of Jesus to come and in doing so activate our faith by making a move. It's when we move and get close to Jesus that things change.

The synagogue ruler was indignant because Jesus healed on the Sabbath. Jesus rebuked him and all his opponents were humiliated. The people, however, were delighted with what Jesus had done. It's not always the religious, the well-educated and the theologically qualified who recognise the hand of God. Such people walked past the man who had been beaten and was cared for by the Good Samaritan. Don't get so caught up in religion, tradition and detail that you miss the point of gospel, which is about Jesus coming to seek and save sinners, the lost, the lonely and isolated.

Today God sees you, your circumstances, your worries, your failings and He says come to me. Find a new posture in Jesus that allows you to look up and to praise the one who set you free.

Reflection on Jesus meeting us at our point of need

Introduction

Jesus, as the 'I Am' of God, was many things to many people in the way He met their specific needs. To the dead Lazarus He was the Resurrection and the Life, to the hungry crowd of 5000 He was the Bread of Life, to Blind Bartimaeus He was The Light of the World and to Zacchaeus He was The Good Shepherd. Because Jesus is the same yesterday, today and for ever (Hebrews 13 v 8), He still meets specific needs. This reflection from John 21 v 1 - 14 helps us to see and appreciate this.

Jesus Sees the Need

Saint John records in his Gospel an incident when Jesus, after His resurrection, appeared to a number of His disciples after they had been out fishing and caught nothing. In terms of the disciples it had been and was a traumatic time. They had come to a point where they were probably at a loss because Jesus was no longer permanently with them in person as he had been. They had no set masterplan in terms of the way ahead and didn't know where Jesus was or if He would ever appear to them again. In many ways they were in limbo, wondering what next.

Because of this uncertainty, it seems they were on the verge of drifting back into their old way of living. They had gathered near the Sea of Tiberias, a place that they were very familiar with as fishermen and without hesitation they followed Peter's lead to go fishing. Saint John tells us that they fished all night but caught nothing. This was in spite of them being experienced fishermen and fishing in a location they knew so well. They were in danger of discovering the truth of Proverbs 29 v 18 where it says, "Where there is no vision the people perish."

A lesson here is that sometimes, due to circumstances and our actions, we feel God has left us, forgot about us and so we are in danger of starting to go backwards in God and having no purpose as a Christian. However, going backwards to old ways, as the disciples discovered, only leads to disappointment, frustration and fruitlessness. After their fruitless and unsuccessful night, the disciples head for shore, probably at a loss, tired, cold, frustrated and hungry. It is at this point Jesus appears to them again, meeting them at their point of need. Although not a fisherman by trade, He instructs them to throw their nets to the other side and they end up having a huge haul of fish. It is then they recognised who He was. I am sure an element of guilt crept in when they recognised Jesus, given what they were doing. However, Jesus didn't condemn or criticise them.

The same Jesus is always looking out for us and comes time and time again at our point of need and weakness. He comes to aid and restore, not to condemn. He can turn our failure and failings into success, no matter what the circumstances or reasons are. All we have to do is obey Him and accept His offer of help, taking comfort in knowing that He will never leave or forsake us. It is then we will recognise Jesus in a fresh new light.

Jesus Meets Physical Need.

Jesus knew where to find the disciples and so he came to the shore to meet and encounter them. Because of who He is, He also knows where we are every moment of every day and willingly comes to our aid in times of need. Without being told, Jesus knew the disciples had physical needs after a long unsuccessful night of fishing. He knew they were hungry, tired, frustrated and cold. And so Jesus met them at their point of physical need as he had a fire going and was preparing a breakfast of cooked fish and bread for them. Jesus wasn't too aloof or proud to get His hands dirty. It was when they obeyed His instruction that they gained success and recognised Him.

I am sure His action of cooking breakfast and serving the disciples brought back memories of when He had served them not long before His arrest and had washed their feet. Maybe the bread and fish reminded them of Jesus feeding the 5000. As Jesus cooked, He asked them to bring some fish also, showing the disciples that they still had a role and that Jesus wanted them to work in partnership with Him. He still wanted them to be 'fishers of men'.

Just as Jesus was concerned about the physical welfare of the disciples, so He is concerned about our physical welfare. He knows if we are weary and struggling. He knows if we have problems about work or finances. He knows if we are struggling with illness. Just as He met the disciples at their point of physical need and provided what they needed, He will do the same for us if we listen to Him and follow His instruction.

Jesus Meets Emotional Need.

As well as their physical need, Jesus knew the disciples had emotional needs. I am sure they felt guilt, sadness and shame at the way they had run away and even denied Jesus at His point of need. They were probably emotionally drained and fearful because they didn't know what the future held. Even as fishermen they had been unsuccessful during the night, not being able to catch any fish. They must have felt like failures and were frustrated. Maybe depression had set in and darkness clouded their thinking and judgement.

However, when Jesus came He allowed them to be successful again and restored their pride. All it took was some humility (acknowledging they didn't have the answers) and some obedience (recognising someone else knew better and responding). When His instruction was followed they caught so many fish they couldn't haul them into the boat. He set their minds at rest by calling them friends and showing that He was not there to judge or condemn, but to restore.

Jesus wants us to be emotionally sound. He comes to dispel fear, shame and guilt and so he offers forgiveness time and time again. Jesus wants us to be successful and to feel good about ourselves, not just in terms of our physical lives but in every aspect of our lives. I left school with seven GSE's (GCSE's in today's speak). I didn't go to university but started work aged seventeen. I believe God directed my path so much so that I ended up as part of a senior management team in a highly successful international company, having significant responsibilities for finance, human resources and business improvement. Many times in my career I was faced with tasks that I struggled with, causing me anxiety and stress. Many times I felt emotionally drained. But each time at my point of need, God would step and help me to avoid failure and to be successful. Jesus will do the same for you if you will let Him.

Jesus Meets Spiritual Need.

When Jesus came to meet the disciples, they weren't found in prayer, they weren't fasting and they certainly weren't having a revival meeting. Rather they had gone fishing, which had been their old way of living. They were probably wondering what the future held. Jesus wasn't physically with them to provide guidance and instruction. Their faith had taken a beating. They had no plan of action and hence slipping back into their old way of living was a real possibility. Jesus saw the disciples returning to shore and knew where they were spiritually and that they didn't recognise Him. When there is a loss of communication with Jesus, vision and faith fade. However, in spite of where the disciples where spiritually, Jesus wasn't angry or annoyed with them because they had gone fishing and weren't engaged in spiritual activity. He didn't shout at them or scold them. He simply called out to them, "Friends, haven't you any fish?" When they said, "No," He told them to throw their nets to the right side of the boat and they would catch some. When they followed His instruction they were met with abundant success. It was then the penny dropped and Jesus was recognised.

Can you imagine their joy at encountering Jesus again and knowing that He still worked miracles? His words and direction restored their faith. Their spirits were restored.

Jesus does the same for each of us. He knows where we are spiritually and comes to meet us at our point of need. Maybe our faith has taken a beating. Maybe it has been diluted by circumstances. Maybe we feel Jesus isn't around anymore or doesn't care anymore. Maybe we have turned away and gone backwards. However, Jesus comes to meet us at our point of spiritual need, not to shout or condemn, but to restore our faith and call us friend. Even if we have denied Him and cursed Him, like Peter, Jesus still sees us as friends who are worth restoring. Now, that's good news.

Author Hugh McAllister's contact details: Email: hughmcallister4@gmail.com

CEDRIC
WILSON

Designed & Published by Cedric Wilson
Email: cedricwilson@live.co.uk